Successful Business Plans In A Week

Iain Maitland

The Teach Yourself series has been trusted around the world for over 60 years. This series of 'In A Week' business books is designed to help people at all levels and around the world to further their careers. Learn, in a week, what the experts learn in a lifetime.

Iain Maitland heads up *Property Alerts* news and information websites which include *UK Property Alerts, London Property Alerts* and *International Property Alerts*. He regularly produces business plans for UK and overseas property syndicates and consortia.

Successful Business Plans

Iain Maitland

www.inaweek.co.uk

Hodder Education

338 Euston Road, London NW1 3BH

Hodder Education is an Hachette UK company

First published in UK 1996 by Hodder Education

First published in US 2012 by The McGraw-Hill Companies, Inc.

This edition published 2012

Copyright © 1996, 1998, 2002, 2012 Iain Maitland

The moral rights of the author have been asserted

Database right Hodder Education (makers)

The Teach Yourself name is a registered trademark of Hachette UK.

British Library Cataloguing in Publication Data: a catalogue record for this title is available from the British Library.

Library of Congress Catalog Card Number: on file.

The publisher has used its best endeavours to ensure that any website addresses referred to in this book are correct and active at the time of going to press. However, the publisher and the author have no responsibility for the websites and can make no guarantee that a site will remain live or that the content will remain relevant, decent or appropriate.

The publisher has made every effort to mark as such all words which it believes to be trademarks. The publisher should also like to make it clear that the presence of a word in the book, whether marked or unmarked, in no way affects its legal status as a trademark.

Every reasonable effort has been made by the publisher to trace the copyright holders of material in this book. Any errors or omissions should be notified in writing to the publisher, who will endeavour to rectify the situation for any reprints and future editions.

Hachette UK's policy is to use papers that are natural, renewable and recyclable products and made from wood grown in sustainable forests. The logging and manufacturing processes are expected to conform to the environmental regulations of the country of origin.

www.hoddereducation.co.uk

Typeset by Cenveo Publisher Services.

Printed in Great Britain by CPI Group (UK) Ltd, Croydon, CR0 4YY

Contents

Introduction

All businesses, big and small, established or soon to start, need to know where they are going, both commercially and financially, over the coming months and years. The easiest way to achieve that know-how is to put together a business plan.

What is a business plan?

This is a document that sets out what the business does, or plans to do, where it wants to go, and how it is going to get there, and when. In many ways, it provides a summary of where your business is now, where you want it to be and a framework for going from 'here' to 'there' successfully.

A business plan has many uses. As often as not, it is only ever produced when the business needs to raise finance and a bank asks to see one. It can be used to attract investment in a business, perhaps from a would-be partner. It can also be used to encourage assistance in other ways: to show a prospective landlord, for example, that this is a solid and growing, here-to-stay business.

Surprisingly few entrepreneurs put together a business plan just for their own use – and perhaps this is a contributory factor in so many business failures. If a business does not have a clear idea of what it's doing and where it's going, and a firm grasp of its finances, especially its profit margins and cash flow, it is certainly making it harder for itself to achieve its goals.

What does it consist of?

A business plan usually comprises two, or sometimes three, sections:

A **commercial section** will set out what the business does, the products or services it provides, who's involved with the business, the market it operates in and where it wants to go in the months and years ahead.

How?

2. A **financial section** sets out these commercial activities and objectives in financial terms. It will look at the current financial circumstances, including a profit budget and a cash-flow forecast along with past and projected accounts, and detail any financial requirements.

3. **Appendices** may comprise a third and final section. These will feature a mix of documents from independent third parties which back up and clarify what's been included in the commercial and financial sections. You might find agreements with suppliers in here.

Think dissertation appendices.

How to write it

First time around, the idea of putting together a business plan can be daunting. It should not be. If you are running, or are planning to set up, a business, all the information you need should be known to you or be readily available. If it isn't, it's about time it was!

As with writing all documents or reports, the best way to approach a business plan is to break everything down into smaller parts you can do one at a time. That's why doing a business plan in a week is ideal – you can set aside some time each day to do each part in turn.

This book takes you step by step through the whole process, cutting through the theory and the waffle, to show you how to put together a successful business plan in just seven days...

Iain Maitland

SUNDAY

Understanding business plans

SUNDAY
MONDAY
TUESDAY
WEDNESDAY
THURSDAY
FRIDAY
SATURDAY

Today we will begin by taking an overview of business plans. We've already seen that a business plan comprises a commercial section, a financial section and, sometimes, appendices as well. It would be helpful, before we start writing anything down, even in note form, to consider what we might want to include in each of these sections.

We've talked, too, of the uses of a business plan and the fact that it's often only put together on request – from a bank, a would-be investor or a prospective supplier, for example. However, the greatest, and most often overlooked, use is actually for the business itself.

How we present a business plan – its key features – is important as well. Whether we are submitting a plan by email or in writing, it has to create the correct, professional impression. Some banks, for example, will expect us to fill in a ready-made form which they'll provide. In this case, we may need to employ someone with neat handwriting if ours is a spider's crawl! So, to start us off, we will look more closely at these three areas in particular...

- contents
- uses
- key features.

Contents

Not surprisingly, all business plans are different, but most of them will contain three main sections:
- a commercial section
- a financial section
- appendices.

The commercial section

In this first section, we would normally include some preliminary materials such as a title page, contents page and introduction. These would then be followed by text about our business, products and services, team, market and overall objectives. The names and order of these subjects and the precise information given about them may vary from one plan to another, but they should all be covered in some detail somewhere in this section.

The financial section

Equally important, if not more so in some instances, the financial section of a business plan will usually incorporate a profit budget and cash-flow forecast indicating the estimated profits and ongoing cash position within the firm over a given period of time. These will often be accompanied by past or projected – or both – annual accounts, such as a profit and loss account and a balance sheet, plus details of current financial circumstances and requirements.

Appendices

This final section comprises photographs, samples, letters, forms, documents and other items from independent sources which verify and occasionally add to all of the statements, financial facts and figures laid down in the commercial and financial sections. In many respects, these appendices can be viewed as the foundation of a successful business plan:

without them, the preceding text may be seen as little more than unsubstantiated and biased opinions.

Here is a checklist of what we might include in our business plan:

1 Commercial section
- title page
- contents page
- introduction
- the business
- products and services
- the team
- the market
- objectives

2 Financial section
- profit budget
- cash-flow forecast
- past accounts
- future accounts
- current financial circumstances
- financial requirements

3 Appendices
- photographs
- samples
- letters
- forms
- documents
- other items

Uses

We may compile a business plan for various reasons. Most often, it will be used to:

- raise finance
- attract investment
- encourage assistance
- improve performance.

SUNDAY

MONDAY

TUESDAY

WEDNESDAY

THURSDAY

FRIDAY

SATURDAY

Raise finance

If we need funds to start, buy or expand a firm in some way, a plan may be sent to a prospective lender such as a bank manager, charitable trust, venture capital house or even family or friends who have savings or redundancy money available. Hopefully, we can convince the relevant parties both that we have a viable proposal and that we will be able to make capital and interest payments on time.

Attract investment

Similarly, the business plan could be used to attract investment and would, in this case, be written to highlight the firm's forthcoming activities and potential profits and the possible rewards and risks for would-be investors. Such a plan may be forwarded to wealthy individuals and to organizations such as venture capital institutions which specialize in investing in up-and-coming companies, especially those trading in new and innovative activities.

Encourage assistance

Sometimes, we need help from other people and organizations in order to trade successfully and prosper. Perhaps we want a prospective landlord to grant a lease to us, a supplier to enter into a sole agency agreement for our town or a fellow trader to allow us to use their storage and distribution facilities. These parties may be more willing to do what we want if they have been given a plan which outlines both our requirements and intentions and the mutual benefits arising from them.

Improve performance

Even if we do not require external finance, investment or assistance, it is still a good idea to draw up a business plan anyway, for our own internal use. Preparing commercial and financial sections (and appendices where appropriate) enables us to assess our business in an objective manner. We may get to know it better, along with its individual strengths and weaknesses, and be able to set more realistic objectives as a consequence of this increased knowledge and understanding.

Just as significant, a business plan provides us with a commercial and financial framework against which we can regularly compare our performance to see if we are on course to achieve our objectives. Possible problems such as rising costs and imminent cash shortfalls can hopefully be spotted and resolved well in advance. If reviewed and amended at monthly intervals, our plan enables us to monitor, control and improve the overall performance of our business. For many, this is the most important function of a business plan.

Key features

We now have an overview of what a business plan is, what it contains and how we can use it. Next, we need to think about those key features that distinguish a successful business plan from an unsuccessful one. Obviously, we will wish to incorporate these into the plan that we are going to write.

Ideally, our business plan will be:

- well researched
- adapted
- attractive
- understandable
- realistic
- well supported.

SUNDAY

MONDAY

TUESDAY

WEDNESDAY

THURSDAY

FRIDAY

SATURDAY

Well researched

A successful business plan is researched fully, and is only completed once all the commercial, financial and supporting information that may need to be included in it has been gathered together. The plan should create the strong impression that the writer knows everything there is to know and can prove it with independent, backup information.

As soon as the reader thinks of something they wish to see, they should be able to find it. And if they want proof of a statement, it should be readily available from an independent source in the appendices.

Adapted

Of course, not all of the facts and figures that we are going to collect should be put into the plan – otherwise it might run to tens or even hundreds of pages! Its content, structure, emphasis and length must vary according to what our particular reader wants to know about and how much time they have to read it. When writing, look at what the reader will be thinking – in essence – 'What's in it for me?' Show them! For example, a bank wishes to know about commercial activities but only in relation to likely profits, cash flow and financial requirements. They want to get their money back, with interest, and on time. A prospective landlord, on the other hand, may want to learn about how our business and activities might affect other tenants, but little else.

However much information we want to incorporate – and there is no right or wrong length for a business plan – we must try to keep it as brief and to the point as we can. Always asking 'Is this relevant?' before noting anything down should help us to achieve this. The reader will only have a certain amount of time to study our plan, and needs to be able to do it swiftly. We can assist them in doing this by omitting superfluous and repetitive material.

Attractive

Whether it's being submitted online or as hard copy – whichever the reader wants – a winning business plan must have a smart and professional appearance, especially if it is being sent out to raise finance, attract investment or encourage assistance in some way. This will give us an efficient, businesslike image and should put the reader in a more favourable mood towards both us and the proposition that we are making. Clearly, the business proposal itself must still be a viable one if it is to be accepted, but it obviously helps to get the reader on our side as far as possible.

If a hard-copy business plan, it should be put inside a clean and classy-looking file or folder: this not only creates a professional impression but also protects the material from becoming torn and dirty as it is being passed around. We should choose a file which matches our image – colourful and jazzy if we are artistic, plain and dark if we are methodical and serious. For easy identification, it is a good idea to place a white sticker on the front of the file and type (or write neatly) the title of the plan on it along with our name, address, phone/fax number, email address and/or website, and the date. A business logo adds a classy touch, too:

KALEIDOSCOPE
A
BUSINESS PROPOSAL
BY
TOM HUDSON
2, THE COTTAGES, NEWTOWN, SUFFOLK FE7 3BH
TEL/FAX: 01394 770512
E-MAIL: THUDSON@NVC.COM
DATE: 1 MAY 2012

To emphasize our professionalism, a hard-copy plan needs to be on top-quality, A4 paper, perhaps selecting white or another shade if we want to co-ordinate colours to achieve a particular style and image. The text should be typed, rather than handwritten and amateurish, and should be set out carefully. We ought to include generous margins at the top, sides and bottom of each page, plenty of headings and subheadings, short paragraphs of similar length, and bullet points where appropriate. These all help to improve the overall appearance, making it easier to read, and give the reader sufficient room in which to note comments and queries.

Here is an example of what we should be aiming for:

SUNDAY

MONDAY

TUESDAY

WEDNESDAY

THURSDAY

FRIDAY

SATURDAY

About Kaleidoscope

Its purpose

Kaleidoscope is being set up to meet the needs of those families who wish to hire rather than buy nursery goods and equipment, typically overnight and on an occasional basis.

Its location

It will be based in a newly built, 500-square-metre showroom alongside our home. This is within two minutes' walking distance of the town's only health centre, St John's Playgroup and Eyke Primary School (see 'Appendix 2: Eyke Map' on pages 3–4 of the appendices).

Its products and services

Initially, we will stock the following goods:

Moses baskets	baby-bouncers
carrycots	baby-walkers
cribs	highchairs

We should always submit clean, fresh printouts rather than photocopies which would create the impression that this is little more than a circular being sent out to everyone. (We can, however, put extra, clean copies of the plan at the back of our file or folder if we know that several people will wish to study it.) The text must be free from any spelling mistakes, typing errors or inaccuracies such as incorrectly added figures. These will confuse and muddle the reader and damage our reputation. We need to check, check and check again – and then retype, if necessary.

Understandable

Our language must match the reader's knowledge and understanding of the subject matter. We should use clear, simple words and phrases when addressing a lay person who may be bewildered by trade jargon. Likewise, we should incorporate technical expressions where appropriate when writing to an expert who might otherwise feel patronized. The key to success here is to think carefully about what our reader knows and to pitch our language at the right level. It is important that we do not automatically assume they are as familiar with the subject as we are – this is rarely the case.

Whatever we have to say, we must ensure that we use specific words and phrases, rather than vague ones such as 'good', 'nice', 'better than' and 'cheaper than', which will be defined differently by each reader. For example, '£33.95' is understood clearly, whereas 'a good price' means nothing.

Humorous comments and statements must be avoided at all times, too. What we find funny may be interpreted in another way by a person with an alternative sense of humour. Our joke could be seen as flippant and, when finance or investment is being sought, humour is often considered inappropriate.

Realistic

Obviously, we need to sound 100-per-cent confident and enthusiastic about our firm and its prospects – after all, if we are not, we cannot expect the reader to be either! Nevertheless, we must not get too carried away, as this may make us sound naïve and could undermine what we are stating. Most readers will possess some knowledge of what we are writing about, and will be able to distinguish between facts and fantasy.

Our statements and financial figures need to be sensible and achievable. We should base them on solid, reliable evidence such as past income and expenditure and definite sales orders. Prospective difficulties must be addressed fully rather than being glossed over or ignored completely. We should identify and then explain clearly how we are going to overcome, or at least cope with, them. By not referring to them, we simply appear evasive or incompetent. It is sensible to deal in detail only with the immediate future, namely the coming year: the longer ahead we look, the more speculative our comments become. Our reader is more interested in reality than hopes and dreams.

Well supported

A successful business plan always backs up its commercial and financial sections with independent evidence in its appendices. Our comments alone will not be accepted at face value, especially if money is involved. We therefore have to be willing and able to prove everything we say is true by supplying additional, verifying material from reputable sources, and, ideally, independent ones.

Summary

At the end of our first day of work on our business plan, we should have a clear idea of what we are going to produce. We will know whether we are putting together a plan to raise finance, attract investment, encourage assistance and/or improve the performance of our business.

From here, we will have worked out whether we are going to produce a commercial section and a financial section and appendices; and what we will include within each of these sections. The commercial section contains the facts, the financial section contains the figures and the appendices contain the proof; all of which confirms that we are showing the reader facts and figures, not opinions and guesswork.

There's more to a business plan than just the facts, the figures and the proof, however. We want to deliver a plan in the way the reader wants to receive it, whether that's online or offline. We want to tell them what they want to know – the 'What's in it for me?' We need to show that we are well informed, professional and know what we are doing. A successful business plan is well researched, adapted, attractive, understandable, realistic and well supported. Remember, it's not just *what* we say, it's *how* we say it!

SUNDAY

MONDAY

TUESDAY

WEDNESDAY

THURSDAY

FRIDAY

SATURDAY

Fact-check [answers at the back]

We can check our understanding of what we've covered today by answering these multiple-choice questions and then comparing our answers with those at the end of the book.

1. What would we expect to see included in the commercial section?
   - a) Information about the business ☑
   - b) The profit budget ❏
   - c) The cash-flow forecast ❏
   - d) Information about products and services ☑

2. What would we expect to find in the financial section?
   - a) The profit budget ☑
   - b) Samples ❏
   - c) The overall objectives ❏
   - d) Annual accounts ◀

3. What would we expect to see in the appendices?
   - a) Financial requirements ❏
   - b) Samples ☑
   - c) Photographs ☑
   - d) Letters ☑

4. What are the main uses of a business plan?
   - a) Advertising ❏
   - b) To raise finance ☑
   - c) To improve performance ☑
   - d) Marketing ❏

5. What do we provide to prove we know 'everything there is to know'?
   - a) Letters of support from employees ❏
   - b) Plenty of opinions and thoughts on the subject ❏
   - c) Our curriculum vitae ❏
   - d) Independent, backup information ☑

6. What does the reader really want to know?
   - a) Our life story and successes to date ❏
   - b) How the product we're selling is made ❏
   - c) 'What's in it for me?' ☑
   - d) As much as possible about everything ❏

7. What might a 'smart and professional' plan include appearance-wise?
   - a) A clean and classy-looking folder ☑
   - b) Handwritten text, corrected where relevant ❏
   - c) Quality A4 paper ☑
   - d) Detailed and dense text ❏

8. What type of language should we use in the plan?
a) Words and phrases suited to the reader's know-how ☑
b) Humorous comments, whenever possible ☐
c) Specific language ☐
d) Vague words and phrases, when in doubt ☐

9. What should we do about 'prospective difficulties' we've identified in advance?
a) Ignore them completely ☐
b) Mention them vaguely ☐
c) Address them fully ☑
d) Wait and see if the reader spots them ☐

10. Our plan should give the reader the strong impression that it is...?
a) A work in progress ☐
b) Well researched ☑
c) Realistic ☑
d) Well supported ☑

SUNDAY

MONDAY

TUESDAY

WEDNESDAY

THURSDAY

FRIDAY

SATURDAY

MONDAY

Making preparatory notes

SUNDAY

MONDAY

TUESDAY

WEDNESDAY

THURSDAY

FRIDAY

SATURDAY

Now we start the proper work. We've got a clear idea of what we've got to put in our commercial and financial sections and our appendices – so let's go and get it. Much of the information we need will be readily available 'in-house'; it's in our heads or we can get it from our work colleagues or books and records, past accounts, and so on. As we'll see in a minute, asking yourself lots of questions is a good place to begin.

We may not have everything we need to know and include in-house. This is especially true when it comes to putting together the appendices – remember, the material in here needs to back up the facts in the commercial section and the figures in the financial section. As important, it needs to be from *independent* sources. We need to contact these independent sources – banks, customers, and so on. What *they* have to say is as important as what *we* have to say.

The chances are that we are going to generate a great deal of information that could go into this business plan. What we need to do is to be able to pull out the key facts and figures and to decide what we'll discard. We also need to decide what's going to be included in the appendices and what will be left out. We've lots to do today. Let's crack on with...

- conducting internal research
- using external sources
- accumulating appropriate information.

Conducting internal research

Much of the information we need to put into our business plan can be obtained relatively easily, from in-house sources:

- our own knowledge
- our colleagues
- books and records.

Our own knowledge

More often than not, our understanding of the business will be greater than anyone else's. We may have established the firm and perhaps now sell the goods, recruit the team, deal personally with customers, and so on. Who else knows as much as us? Probably nobody! We should therefore draw upon our own background knowledge and information before proceeding further.

One of the best ways of doing this is to ask ourselves lots of questions. Our answers will generate plenty of preparatory notes that we can use as the basis of our plan. Here are some questions to start us off:

- What is our business?
- What does it do?
- Where is it located?

What & Where

- What are the premises like?
- What equipment, machinery and vehicles do we have?
- What do we sell?
- What are our products and services?
- What are our rivals' goods and services?
- Who works for the firm?
- What are their backgrounds?
- What do they do?
- What are their strengths and weaknesses?
- Who are our customers?
- How much do we know about them?
- Who are our competitors?
- What do we know about them?
- What is the marketplace like?
- How much do we know about it?
- What are our personal goals?
- What are our business objectives?
- How have we been doing financially?
- What are our finances like now?
- What will our finances be like in the future?
- What cash will be available?
- What profits will we make in the future?
- How can we prove all this information?

What's
Who's
How's
Where's

How do we tie it all together?!

Our colleagues

In a larger business with various departments for purchasing, production, marketing, administration, personnel and so forth, some of the data required for the plan may have to be obtained by approaching our work colleagues. Whoever we talk to, we do need to be able to distinguish between opinions and facts. Generally, facts are better than opinions, unless the latter come from independent, reputable sources – which our colleagues are not!

Books and records

Whatever the size of our firm, the books and records that we have accumulated so far will be invaluable to us when we are composing our business plan. In particular, we will find it helpful to refer to previous annual accounts, purchase agreements, sales records and orders, and the like. Details can be taken from these and referred to in the text of the plan, with key documents being placed in the appendices for verification.

Normally, most of the facts that we need for the commercial and financial sections of our business plan will be available in-house. However, we need to remember that everything we write about has to be proven, and this usually means obtaining supporting data from outside the firm. Our word alone is not enough: other people's carries more weight.

Using external sources

There are many external sources of information and advice available to us. We should consider all of them, and then approach those which are most likely to be of assistance. The following are usually worth contacting:

How do we back up our plan using those around us?

banks	solicitors
customers	agents
suppliers	associations
competitors	government
accountants	media
	Internet

Banks

As our bank is probably going to receive our plan, it is sensible to get in touch with them beforehand to find out exactly what they want from us and how they want it. Some banks provide ready-made business plan, profit budget and cash-flow forecast forms for us to complete and submit as hard copies or online, and can supply guidance on how to fill these in correctly. Pamphlets and booklets on general business issues and specific details on financial matters are available, too. These all make useful background reading.

BIG PART → what our customers want!

Customers Ultimately our B. Papers them.

Those people and firms who buy our goods and services are an excellent source of advice. They can tell us all we need to know – and to write – about them, including their location, characteristics, wants and needs. In addition, they can give us opinions about our firm and our goods and services which may be useful additions to our appendices. Their comments about our rivals might be revealing as well.

Suppliers

Our suppliers will obviously be able to provide facts and figures about the raw materials, component parts and stocks that we are purchasing from them, along with further, helpful information about mutual customers, competitors and the marketplace. Although some of their additional comments may be biased, these will usually contain one or two points of use to us.

Competitors

Many small businesses compete amicably against each other, with the overall aim of surviving against larger companies trading nearby. If we can establish friendly relationships, we may be able to draw on their knowledge of goods, services, customers and the market. Clearly, we may find out more about them as well, which will enable us then to write about them with greater accuracy.

Accountants

Costly though they are, an accountant can often put us in touch with potential financiers, provide advice on all money matters, help us to write our financial section, and give our business plan a greater veneer of respectability. It is usually wise to choose an accountant on the basis of recommendations from fellow traders we can trust. We need to be aware of the likely costs involved in using them, and evaluate these alongside the possible benefits.

Solicitors

We could approach a solicitor for guidance on legal issues that we need to refer to in our plan – partnership agreements, contracts of sale, freehold deeds, leasehold agreements and planning permission, among other items. As with an accountant, we should make our choice from personal recommendations and compare the expense against the advantages of referring to them. Evidently, they are invaluable in some instances.

Agents

Business transfer agents who specialize in selling going concerns will be able to supply data about businesses for sale, what to look for and how to value them, as well as information about freehold and leasehold properties, and how to agree rents – all potential text for the different sections of our plan. Similarly, estate agents can comment on freehold and leasehold premises, prices, rents and rates in our region, which may be of some value to our business plan.

Associations

Local chambers of commerce or trade run by business people in the community can be a good source of off- and on-the-record advice about what is happening in the area. Representative associations in our trade or industry can provide or verify much of the commercial information needed. Membership of a nationwide, small-business association confers many benefits for members, including an advisory service on most business issues.

Government

Our local council can be a helpful source of information on such subjects as low-cost finance and grants available, planning permission procedures and forthcoming developments. Some councils even employ small-business advisers who can assist in the writing of business plans. A variety of statistics, surveys and reports are continually being produced by national government and supplied through its departments. Many of these contain useful background details for our plan.

Media

Newspapers, magazines and websites may have included articles about our business, products, services, employees, customers and competitors at some time in the past. We may find it beneficial to refer to these once more when compiling our commercial section in particular. Copies of recent articles could then be placed within the appendices to support any comments made. Don't forget to search for information online, via www.google.com etc.

Here are some other sources of potential use to us:

architects	printers
surveyors	insurance brokers
illustrators	libraries
photographers	market research companies

Accumulating appropriate information

We now need to start sorting through the mass of information that has come to us from all the different sources, making notes which subsequently can form the basis of our business plan. We could use these headings:

- The business
- Products and services
- The team
- The market
- Objectives
- Finance
- Appendices

The business

Under this heading, we could jot down notes about our firm or business idea, including whatever we think is most relevant in our situation. Typically, we might write about its history, activities and current position, location and premises, equipment, machinery and vehicles. It is up to us to decide what our reader wants to see and to include it.

Products and services

Here, we might note down information about the numbers and types of products and services that we offer, along with their main features and selling points. It is important to make notes too about rival goods and services, comparing and contrasting these with our own. We need to be especially realistic at this point, being aware of our shortcomings and how we are going to deal with them.

The team

Beneath this heading, we should focus on ourselves as well as on our colleagues and employees, as appropriate. In particular, we should note our individual careers to date, skills, knowledge, experiences, strengths and weaknesses, and how we all fit together to form a good team.

The market

Here, we should concentrate on our customers – their numbers, types, locations and purchasing habits. We need to make notes about our competitors, too – numbers, types, locations, activities, strengths and weaknesses. We could also take a broader look at the marketplace itself, especially its size, changes and developments taking place, and future prospects.

Objectives

It is a good idea for us to write out our personal and business objectives for the short, medium and long term – for the next year, three years and thereafter. We must be cautious, though: a lender will want to see that we are not being over-optimistic.

Finance

If we are planning to include a financial section for a bank or whoever, we should sketch out some preliminary notes about our finances to date, likely future sales, costs and profits, and possible forthcoming cash flow into and out of our account, as well as our current financial circumstances and requirements. If we are trying to raise finance, these notes are essential – indeed, as important as all of the other notes put together.

Appendices

Below this final heading, we should make a note of those items which we can put in to back up our statements. Here is a list, in no particular order, of what we might decide to include:

- press cuttings
- certificates/diplomas
- map
- partnership-agreement documents
- property particulars
- photographs of equipment
- company-formation documents
- product samples
- sales records
- suppliers' price lists
- sales orders
- our price lists
- quotes/estimates of costs
- sales literature
- competitors' price lists
- annual accounts
- competitors' sales literature
- proof of security
- accountant's/solicitor's comments
- curricula vitae.

Of course, this does not mean we have to include all of these items – we should consider them all carefully, and then select the relevant ones, placing them in the most appropriate order, section by section.

Summary

Today should have been a hectic day and we should be feeling tired but happy – we've now got lots of information, notes and materials that we can use in our business plan. There may seem to be too much of it and we may not quite know what to do next, but everything is now in place ready to be cut, shaped and trimmed into the perfect business plan.

This may be a good time to just reflect on what we've done today to make sure we have covered everything. A common mistake made by successful entrepreneurs who've set up and run a business from scratch by themselves is to assume that they have all the knowledge needed to put into a winning business plan. But others – customers, suppliers, etc. – may tell us one or two things we didn't know.

Similarly, we need other people and firms to provide us with the backup materials for the appendices. We should, therefore, check that we have referred to colleagues, books and records and used external sources to add to and verify the information we have gathered together. We can then organize all of this into sections – about the business, products and services, team, market, objectives, finance and appendices.

SUNDAY
MONDAY
TUESDAY
WEDNESDAY
THURSDAY
FRIDAY
SATURDAY

Fact-check [answers at the back]

Let's double-check what we've covered today by answering these multiple-choice questions. We can then compare what we've put with the correct answers at the end of the book.

1. Who should know our business best?
   a) Us ☐
   b) Our employees ☐
   c) Our bank manager ☐
   d) Our customers ☐

2. What information do we want from our colleagues?
   a) Facts ☐
   b) Opinions ☐
   c) Figures ☐
   d) Hearsay ☐

3. What books and records should we be accessing for research purposes?
   a) Diaries ☐
   b) Sales records ☐
   c) Christmas card lists ☐
   d) Annual accounts ☐

4. What might we ask our customers about?
   a) Themselves ☐
   b) Their finances ☐
   c) Us ☐
   d) Our plans ☐

5. What might we use an accountant for?
   a) To help us write the commercial section ☐
   b) To find sources of finance ☐
   c) To help us with the financial facts and figures ☐
   d) To compile the appendices for us ☐

6. What might our solicitor deal with?
   a) Partnership agreements ☐
   b) Profit budgets ☐
   c) Freehold and leasehold matters ☐
   d) Cash-flow forecasts ☐

7. Business transfer agents can provide us with information about...
   a) Businesses for sale? ☐
   b) Business valuations? ☐
   c) Sources of finance? ☐
   d) Online marketing? ☐

8. What headings would we include when making notes about the business?
   a) Activities ☐
   b) Location ☐
   c) Premises ☐
   d) Finances ☐

9. What headings would we include when making notes about the market?
   a) History ☐
   b) Customers ☐
   c) Staff ☐
   d) Competitors ☐

10. What headings would feature among those for notes about our finances?
    a) Staff ☐
    b) Costs ☐
    c) Profits ☐
    d) Cash flow ☐

TUESDAY

Composing the commercial section

Today we're going to get down to doing some writing. It doesn't have to be perfect as it's not going to be 'set in stone' at this stage. But we do want to start taking all of that preparatory work and materials and sorting it all into some sort of order.

We will start with the commercial section. This is, in many ways, the driving force of our business plan as it sets out what it is, what it does, where it is going and when. All the other parts of the plan really back up this first section. The main headings in the commercial section are 'Our business', 'Our products and services', 'Our team', 'The market' and 'Our objectives'. Before we get going on any writing, we may want to just sort our notes and materials into these areas.

Whether we are submitting the plan online or as hard copy, according to the recipient's wishes, being able to write it on screen in the first instance is ideal as we can edit it easily, move text around, trim it down and so on. We are just going to draft everything without worrying too much about style and phrasing. For now, we will sketch out the contents under these headings...

- the preliminaries
- our business
- our products and services
- our team
- the market
- our objectives.

The preliminaries

The commercial section should begin with:

1 a title page
2 a contents page
3 an introduction.

The title page

This should simply repeat the information given on the file or folder in which the business plan is being submitted. Restating its title plus our name, address, telephone/fax number, email address and/or website and the date of compilation will ensure that the plan is instantly recognizable if it is separated from its file.

The contents page

Whoever is studying our business plan will wish to be able to find relevant topics promptly. Thus, a precise and accurate list of contents must be included showing the order of the various subjects we have dealt with and the respective pages to be referred to. We need to draft the contents page and number all of the pages after we have completed the entire plan. If we do it any earlier, we will then inevitably think of two or three other items which need to be put somewhere in the text. Renumbered pages – with '11a' and '11b' slotted in and '12' rewritten as '13' and so on – look sloppy and convey a slapdash image. We must avoid this at all costs.

The introduction

We should never underestimate the significance of an introduction: it can mean the difference between success and failure. Bankers, prospective investors and other interested parties will probably be busy, with little time to study every business plan sent to them. Their initial impression of our plan therefore will decide whether it receives either their full, undivided attention or no more than a cursory glance before rejection.

To convince the recipient that our plan deserves to be studied, we should broadly summarize the text. We might say what our business is selling, who our customers are and what objectives we have. Most important of all to the reader, we must then explain what it is that we want them to do for us – provide finance, supply goods or whatever.

Ideally, we will also point out what is in it for them if they do help us – after all, that, more than anything else, is going to persuade them to read on! Remember the phrase, 'What's in it for me?' That's what most readers are thinking as they read.

As with the contents page, we should write the introduction once we have finished the rest of the plan – otherwise we will only have to redo it if we subsequently decide to change the order of the subjects. Looking at each section in turn, 'Our business', 'Products and services' and so forth, we should sum them up in one or two sentences. If these are all then put together and trimmed to remove vague and repetitive comments, we should have a first-rate introduction which is both brief and informative.

Our business

With our earlier notes to hand, we can start writing about the business, in particular:

- its background
- its location
- its premises.

The background

If the business has been trading for some time, we should set out its track record to date – when, where and why it was launched, how it has progressed to reach its current position, its achievements and the obstacles overcome. If we are buying a business, we should say why it is for sale – and the reason should be the *real* one, which may not necessarily be the same as that given by the vendor! On the other hand, we could be getting ready to start a business from scratch. If so, we must supply background information about our ideas instead – what made us think of this business, why we believe it will be successful, how, where and when we will start trading. Everything we write down should be supported by substantiating evidence – balance sheets, profit and loss accounts, a business transfer agent's details, an accountant's letter, newspaper and magazine clippings and the like.

The location

We should write about the location, too – the reasons for basing the business there, its advantages, and its disadvantages and how we are working to overcome them. We must also mention any anticipated changes taking place in the locality, such as a new factory or road, and state how we will deal with the opportunities and challenges that arise as a result.

An excellent way of supporting this text is to slot a map into the appendices. On this, we should highlight the locations of our business, suppliers, customers, competitors and other key data such as influential neighbours and any attractions which draw people into the area, such as free car parks. Sometimes, it can be helpful to include two maps: one a close-up of the firm and its immediate vicinity; the other a map of the town or trading region.

The premises

If we are buying a property, we should note the asking price, the amount of capital we have to invest, why we want to buy instead of rent and what we will do if the business fails. We must be realistic here. If we are renting, we should refer to any premium we will have to pay, the amount and frequency of rental payments, service charges and the date of the next rent review. Again, we must say what we will do with the lease if the business is unsuccessful.

Next, we should specify the dimensions of our premises and the internal and external layouts, plus the equipment, machinery and vehicles used. We need to explain whether these are owned or leased, how long they will last, when we will need to replace them and what they are and will be worth.

Again, it is essential that we substantiate everything we have stated to prove it is all true. We might think about putting in the estate agent's particulars, a copy of the freehold deeds or leasehold agreement, the solicitor's and surveyor's reports, and photographs and diagrams of equipment, machinery and vehicles, as appropriate.

Our products and services

Going on with this section, we should concentrate on detailing our products and services as appropriate – more specifically:

- their main features
- their unique selling points.

The main features

We must state what our products and services are and how they contribute towards our stock and sales levels. We should outline what these products look like, how they work and what they can be used for. With services, we must state what they involve us doing for customers. It may be a good idea to explain how we make or buy our goods – production processes, output and quality control, suppliers, terms and conditions of sale.

We should also mention our prices plus any discounts offered for bulk buys or prompt payments, saying why goods and services are priced at that level, and showing them to be competitively priced *and* profitable. It is important to write about advertising and selling methods, too – how we advertise and sell our products and services, why our choices are effective, who sells our goods, how they are distributed, and so on.

We then have to decide what verifying documents should be included in the appendices. It is useful to put in photographs, illustrations and newspaper cuttings – even samples of our goods, if there is room for them. As relevant, we could also include production schedules, suppliers' price lists, letters or invoices stating costs, our price guide and advertising and promotional materials.

The unique selling points

If our products and services are to sell, they must have some obvious advantages over competing goods. Thus, we should provide a short list of our main rivals, with brief descriptions of each of them. We need to put the same type of information about our rivals into the appendices as we did for our own products and services – photos, price lists and sales and advertising literature are a must. Adding samples is a sound idea as well, as appropriate.

It is important to highlight the advantages that our goods have over competing ones *and* how these will be maintained. Being realistic, we must also refer to any disadvantages that our products and services may have, explaining how we intend to remedy them. A timetable showing when the changes and improvements will be made may be a useful addition to the business plan.

Our team

When composing the commercial section, we must never forget to detail the most important ingredient of any business: the people within it – that means us! Therefore, we should make sure that we include one or two paragraphs about:

● ourselves
● colleagues and employees.

Ourselves

It is often said that most financiers and investors are primarily backing the people involved, with money and assistance being provided on the strength of their personalities, skills, knowledge, experiences and finances. Every statement we make about ourselves must indicate that we have what it takes to be successful!

It is probably best to approach this part of the text in a chronological order, working forward from, briefly, our school or college days through our career or business history up to the present time. We need to verify our comments with a curriculum vitae, photocopies of certificates and diplomas, press cuttings and even congratulatory letters about our work from former employers or satisfied customers. Let's not hide our light under a bushel!

Colleagues and employees

We should describe our business colleagues in the same way that we wrote about ourselves, outlining their careers to date, drawing in personalities, skills and so forth, and saying what they'll be doing for the firm. If we are jointly controlling a business, it is sensible to discuss the key points of our partnership agreement, how much capital is being introduced by each person, the salaries to be paid, how profits and losses will be shared out, the length of the partnership and how it can be dissolved.

We can then refer to our key employees, such as managers, detailing their past and present jobs plus future roles in the business. After this, we could list the remaining employees, perhaps by name, job title and duties. If there are many of them, it is wiser to state the numbers employed in each department instead. We must not forget to mention the wages we pay to them, either per employee or per department. If we have to buy in any services that cannot be done in-house, we should refer to these here as well, along with a note of the expenses involved.

Relevant documents for our appendices would include curricula vitae of key personnel, copies of certificates and diplomas, partnership agreements and company-formation documents plus written estimates of likely professional fees – in short, anything that will back up what we have just put down in writing.

The market

Ever conscious of our preparatory notes, we can press ahead and write about the marketplace, and most notably:

- the customers
- the competitors.

The customers

If there are not too many of them, we should supply key customers' names and addresses, either here or in the appendices, as appropriate. Alternatively, we can identify them generally in terms of sex, age, income and occupation (or a combination of these). It is sensible to say how many there are, where they are located and how much, and when and why, they will buy from us. We can then discuss the market as a whole plus our share of this. It is advisable to explain how these circumstances may change in the future, and how we will deal with these developments.

We should substantiate the comments we have made about our customers by incorporating documents such as sales records, orders and a map showing where they are. It is wise to support our statements about the market by obtaining matching assessments from reliable, independent sources: chambers of commerce, trade associations and the like.

The competitors

We ought to supply a thumbnail sketch of each competitor in terms of their history, activities, location, premises, goods, customers and market share. Being realistic, we need to say how they are better than us and how we intend to cancel out these advantages. Also, we should state how they are less successful than we are and what we are going to do to keep ahead of them.

As always, we have to back our comments with hard evidence. We should slip into the appendices a website address if appropriate, any newspaper cuttings about their recent activities, successes and failures, a map showing where they are based, photographs of their premises, and sales literature, too. We must prove that what we have stated is a true and fair assessment and not just our personal, biased opinion.

Our objectives

The recipient now has all the key commercial details. However, we still have some important information to put across and it can make the difference between our success or failure. We need to set out our objectives – our plans and intentions for the next year, three years and beyond. The key to success is to be realistic. All of the good work done so far will be undone if we get too carried away. We conclude this commercial section – and today's work – by setting out our objectives. We can divide these as follows:

- the short term,
- the medium term
- the long term.

The short term

The short term covers the next year; it is the immediate future. These goals are easy to set out as we have already talked about them in the commercial section. Read back over what has been written so far. It is a good idea to write them down so that we can prioritize them in their order of importance to us. It is essential that these are all achievable. Too many entrepreneurs seek to impress by 'talking big', deliberately exaggerating what they expect to achieve in order to impress. But most banks, for example, have heard it all before. They are more interested in reality than pipedreams.

The recipient will be interested in facts and figures. So we should take each of our goals and show how it will be achieved. If we say we are aiming for a certain turnover, we should refer to our financial forms to show how we will build up to this.

Whenever we write anything, we must always think how we can back it up. A comment or assurance that is not supported in any way is not worth making. Anyone can say, 'I'll have the biggest business in town next year', but this is meaningless unless it is supported by hard facts and figures.

The medium term

This period of time covers the two years after the first year – the second and third year in business. It is an often overlooked fact that most businesses fail in the first three years, and most of those in the first year itself. In light of this, we should be toning down any thoughts we might have about world domination! It is sensible to have sown the seeds of later success in our short-term goals.

In the medium term, we should be looking to build cautiously on these short-term goals. What many entrepreneurs do wrong is to leap from 'starting up' to, say, 'owning a chain of shops' in the medium term. But a lot needs to happen in between for this to be realized. Taking a shop as an example, we should be thinking about learning 'what's what' in that first year. In the medium term, we should be thinking about testing new lines, with a view to opening a second shop in due course. However, we should not do this until we are ready to do so.

The long term

The long term begins in three years – and goes on indefinitely! It is sensible here to sketch out our overall goals – to have several shops, for example. But we need to couch these in realistic and cautious terms. In business, three years is a long time and most recipients will know that all sorts of things can happen in that time. They will want to see where we are going in general terms, but will not expect us to back it up with facts and figures as it is too far away. We should keep these goals in proportion to what is happening now. If we are seeking funds to start a shop, having one or two other shops nearby sounds realistic. A shop in every town all over the country is not.

If the reader isn't interested in seeing a financial section – perhaps a would-be landlord just wants to check that our commercial activities won't clash with those of our fellow tenants – then we will conclude the text here. Being concise, we could possibly remind the recipient what it is we want from them, and how this will both help us to reach our objectives and benefit them as well. Tell them what's in it for them.

SUNDAY

MONDAY

TUESDAY

WEDNESDAY

THURSDAY

FRIDAY

SATURDAY

Summary

We should now have completed the basics of the commercial section; we have taken the mass of information and material we have gathered together and sorted it into some order. What we want to include is now in place and in the right order and all it needs is a tweak and a tidy before it's ready for submission to the bank, a would-be lender or whoever.

It's worth checking that we have included everything and are happy with it. The preliminaries should include a title page, a contents page and an introduction. 'Our business' should cover its background, location and premises. 'Products and services' should describe their features and main selling points. 'Our team' should include sections on ourselves, our colleagues and our employees. 'The market' should touch upon the market, customers and competitors. 'Our objectives' should be broken down into the short, medium and long term.

Going over what we've written at this stage is helpful. Already, we will probably see text where we've written a little too much or possibly repeated ourselves. The reader wants to read what we've written quickly – so we need to just include the key facts and state them as succinctly as we can. We've a little editing to do as and when we reread –but not yet. We need to go on and put together our financial section first.

SUNDAY

MONDAY

TUESDAY

WEDNESDAY

THURSDAY

FRIDAY

SATURDAY

Fact-check [answers at the back]

We can check Tuesday's work by answering these multiple-choice questions. We can then see the correct answers at the end of the book.

1. What should we include in the preliminary part of the commercial section?
   - a) Title page ❑
   - b) Curriculum vitae ❑
   - c) Contents page ❑
   - d) Introduction ❑

2. When should we write the introduction?
   - a) First of all ❑
   - b) As we go along ❑
   - c) At the end ❑
   - d) Not at all ❑

3. Which of these sections should feature in 'Our business'?
   - a) Background ❑
   - b) Marketing ❑
   - c) Objectives ❑
   - d) Location ❑

4. What should we include when writing about our products' and services' main features?
   - a) Prices ❑
   - b) Selling methods ❑
   - c) Weaknesses ❑
   - d) Sales levels ❑

5. What should we cover when writing about our products' and services' unique selling points?
   - a) Rival goods and services ❑
   - b) Our products' and services' shortcomings ❑
   - c) Costs of selling our products and services ❑
   - d) Timetable of improvements for what we sell ❑

6. 'Our team' section should feature information about...?
   - a) Ourselves ❑
   - b) Our solicitor ❑
   - c) Our accountant ❑
   - d) Our employees ❑

7. What should we include when writing about our customers?
   - a) Their numbers ❑
   - b) Their locations ❑
   - c) Our market share ❑
   - d) Our business objectives ❑

8. What should we include in our comments about our competitors?
   - a) Thumbnail sketches of each competitor ❑
   - b) Their strengths and weaknesses ❑
   - c) Our strengths and weaknesses ❑
   - d) Our customer database ❑

9. Our short-term objectives cover what period of time?
   - a) Just the next month ❑
   - b) Only the next quarter ❑
   - c) Up to the next year ❑
   - d) Up to the next three years ❑

10. Which term(s) should best describe our long-term objectives?
   - a) Realistic ❑
   - b) Full of facts and figures ❑
   - c) Detailed and specific ❑
   - d) Cautious ❑

WEDNESDAY

Compiling the financial section

It's numbers day today – we are putting together the financial section of the plan. This is the part of the plan that would-be lenders and investors are going to look at most closely – they want to know what we want to borrow and how and when we are going to pay it back with interest. All of our numbers have to make sense, add up and be backed up.

It's tempting, if we are not using a business plan to raise finance, to exclude the financial section. This is a mistake that some entrepreneurs make. To be blunt, every entrepreneur should be putting together various financial documents and monitoring them and updating them regularly. How much profit have we made this past quarter? Will we have sufficient cash in place for the rent at the end of next month? These sorts of figures need to be at our fingertips.

We also need to be conscious of the difference between 'profit' and 'cash flow'. A shopkeeper may feel successful because there is always ready cash in the till but this does not mean the shop has sufficient sales to be truly profitable long term. Similarly, a small manufacturer may make lots of sales but takes so long to get paid that it doesn't have enough cash to pay its own bills. We need to produce various documents which reveal...

- a profit budget
- a cash-flow forecast
- annual accounts
- financial requirements.

The profit budget

This budget is concerned with how profitably the firm is trading (or not) – an example of a profit-budget form is shown in Table 1. The budget can be broken down into various parts and tackled accordingly:

- sales
- direct costs
- overheads
- profits
- explanatory notes
- supporting documents.

Sales

We have already anticipated our sales income for the coming year and commented on it in our commercial section. We should now write out our estimated monthly sales in the budget boxes across the form. It is important that we record these sales when we expect them to be made rather than paid for as we are concentrating here on whether or not the business is making sufficient money. The timings of income and expenditure and their effects on our cash resources are looked at later when we tackle the cash-flow forecast.

Direct costs

Direct – or 'variable' – costs fluctuate directly in line with the number of goods produced and sold: the higher the level of sales, the higher the direct costs – and vice versa. There are two main categories of direct cost: 'materials' covers expenditure on raw materials, component parts, packaging and deliveries, while 'wages' refers to the sums paid to production-line workers, sales representatives and the like. We need to note the monthly amounts involved here in the appropriate budget columns. Deducting direct costs from sales leaves us with our 'gross profit'.

Table 1: Profit budget form

	Month:		Month:		Month:		Month:		Month:		Month:		Totals:	
	Budget	Actual	Budget	Actual	Budget	Actual	Budget	Actual	Budget	Actual	Budget	Actual	Budget	Actual
Sales														
Less: materials														
wages														
Gross profit														
Overheads: salaries														
Rent, rates, water														
Insurance														
Repairs, renewals														
Heat, light, power														
Postage														
Printing, stationery														
Transport														
Telephone														
Professional fees														
Depreciation														
Interest charges														
Other														
Total overheads														
Trading profit														

Overheads

These are those fixed items of expenditure such as rent and rates which have to be paid come what may, however many goods are being produced or sold. We need to add up the estimated annual cost of each category of overhead, divide the total by 12 and place the resulting monthly figures in the correct boxes. Remember, we are focusing here on profit, not cash flow. Totting up the various entries in the monthly columns gives us our 'total overheads'. Subtracting these from our gross profit leaves us with our 'trading profit'.

Profits

Our gross and trading profit figures are very important to us. The gross profit figure shows how efficiently we are buying, manufacturing and selling goods. Our 'gross profit margin' can be calculated by dividing gross profit by sales and multiplying by 100. The resulting figure can then be compared with the trade average and conclusions can be drawn about our performance. The trading profit figure, in turn, tells us if the business is truly profitable, and, if so, whether or not satisfactory levels of profit are being achieved.

Explanatory notes

The profit budget is only as good as its explanatory notes. After all, we may know why we have included certain figures, but the bank or whoever else is studying it might not – so we need to tell them. Thus, we should put '1', '2', '3' next to 'Sales', 'Materials', 'Wages' and so on, and attach one or two typed A4 sheets which set out each item on a point-by-point basis and explain how we arrived at our figures. We have to convince the reader that what we've put will be correct. Here are two examples of what we could write:

10 Postage

We have budgeted to spend £20 per week on general correspondence with existing and prospective customers. This is in line with last year's spending – see 'Appendix 6, Annual Accounts', pages 13–14.

11 Printing/stationery

Westbridge Printing will supply us with their standard
pack of letterheads, compliment slips, business cards
and envelopes at a cost of £520. Refer to 'Appendix 7,
Miscellaneous Quotes', pages 15–22.

Supporting documents

Wherever possible, figures and explanatory notes must
be backed up by hard, independent evidence. We need to
accumulate items such as sales orders, suppliers' price lists,
estimates and quotations as we go along, referring to them in
our notes and including them in our accompanying appendices.
Ideally, everything we mention here should be verified in the
appendices by another person or organization of some standing.

The cash-flow forecast

It is essential that a business not only makes a profit but always
has enough cash reserves available to pay the bills and keep
trading comfortably. A business can be profitable on paper but
still fail because it does not get enough cash in on time to pay
its bills. Cash flow is often as important as profitability.

A cash-flow forecast shows how money flows into and out of
a firm over a given period of time. An example of a typical form
is shown in Table 2. The forecast can be viewed in several ways,
but the following elements must be involved in its completion:

- receipts
- payments
- balances
- supplementary notes
- backup materials.

Receipts

Incomings will probably derive from three main sources: capital
introduced by us, cash from sales made, and cash from debtors
(those people or organizations which owe us money). We need

Table 2: Cash-flow forecast

	Month.		Month.		Month.		Month.		Month.		Totals.	
	Budget	Actual	Budget	Actual	Budget	Actual	Budget	Actual	Budget	Actual	Budget	Actual
Receipts: capital												
Cash from sales												
Cash from debtors												
Total receipts (A)												
Payments: creditors												
Salaries, wages												
Rent, rates, water												
Insurance												
Repairs, renewals												
Heat, light, power												
Postage												
Printing, stationery												
Transport												
Telephone												
Professional fees												
Capital payments												
Interest charges												
Other												
VAT payable												
Total payments (B)												
Net cash flow (A-B)												
Opening bank balance												
Closing bank balance												

to note the relevant amounts in the appropriate budget boxes according to when we expect the money to be *received*. We ought to be rather pessimistic here as it will often be much later than anticipated. Totting up each month's budgeted receipts enables us to complete our 'total receipts' line.

Payments

Most of the relevant information here can be lifted from our profit budget but amended to take account of the timings of outgoings – which will hopefully occur *after* incomings so that a healthy cash flow is maintained at all times. Adding up each month's budgeted payments then allows us to write out the 'total payments' line.

Balances

If we deduct our total monthly receipts from payments, we will be left with our 'net cash-flow': and this should be a positive rather than a negative sum if we are operating a cash-conscious firm. As relevant, we then add or subtract this amount to or from our 'opening bank balance', which gives us our 'closing bank balance', for the month. This figure then becomes the opening bank balance for the next month, and so on across to the 'totals' column on the right-hand side of the form.

Supplementary notes

All too often, banks are sent a highly detailed forecast and are then expected to interpret it correctly without any help. Evidently, this is difficult to do, and will not put the reader in a good mood towards us. As with the profit budget, we should therefore note, '1', '2', '3' and so forth down the side of the form and explain the figures point by point on attached A4 sheets of paper.

Backup materials

Similarly, we need to prove as far as possible that what we have forecasted will actually happen over the coming months. The best way of doing this is to refer to backup materials, such as loan agreement forms, letters from debtors and suppliers' terms of sale, and to include these in the appendices. Our own word and opinions are not enough proof: we need to substantiate these with comments and statements from other, independent people and firms.

Annual accounts

Having spent some time calculating our finances over the next year, it is a good idea to look at where we will be financially at that time. We can do this by drawing up two statements from the data accumulated so far:

- a profit and loss account
- a balance sheet.

The profit and loss account

This financial statement summarizes the sales, total costs and profits or losses of a firm over a specific period of time, usually one year. This statement is easy to put together as almost all of the relevant information can be taken from our profit budget. We must remember, however, to deal only with invoiced income and expenditure here – when the bills are actually paid is disregarded. As appropriate, one or two explanatory notes may need to be added for clarification purposes.

Here is an example of a profit and loss account:

Sales		368,327
Opening stock	42,322	
Purchases	127,400	
Closing stock	44,170	
Cost of sales		125,552
Gross profit		242,775

Overheads:

Salaries/wages	67,528	
Rent/rates/water	36,240	
Insurance	5,750	
Repairs/renewals	2,300	
Heat/light/power	1,060	
Postage	1,030	
Printing/stationery	1,260	
Transport	1,241	
Telephone	860	
Depreciation	752	
Total		118,021
Net profit		124,754

The balance sheet

Our second statement shows our firm's assets and liabilities at a given time and indicates how its activities have been funded. Normally, a balance sheet will be drawn up at yearly intervals alongside a profit and loss account. Much of the data contained within it can be lifted from our profit-budget and cash-flow forecast forms.

Here is an example of a balance sheet:

Fixed assets		159,600
Current assets:		
Stock	32,300	
Debtors	5,750	
Cash	5,620	
	43,670	

Current liabilities:		
Overdraft	2,600	
Creditors	9,720	
	12,320	
Net current assets		31,350
Net assets		190,950
Funded by:		
Owners' capital		45,000
Bank loan		45,000
Profit		100,950
		190,950

'Fixed assets' are those permanent items of long-term value, such as land, buildings, equipment and machinery. Of greater day-to-day concern are the 'current assets', which are the ever-changing items, such as stock, debtors and cash, that come and go during trading. 'Current liabilities', such as a bank overdraft and debts to suppliers, need to be settled in the near future, usually within 12 months. Subtracting current liabilities from current assets leaves us with our 'net current assets' (or 'net current liabilities' as the case may be). Adding or deducting these to or from our fixed assets produces our overall 'net assets' (or again, possibly, 'net liabilities').

Under or alongside these figures, we need to show what the firm's activities have been 'funded by'. Here, we might incorporate items such as our own capital, bank loans and profit from our profit and loss account. The total sum should be the same as that for net assets – hence the word 'balance' in the term 'balance sheet'. Again, we might add one or two supplementary comments at the bottom of the statement, just to clarify or expand on entries, as necessary.

Financial requirements

If the business plan is being prepared for a prospective lender, this is their need-to-know information. We have to tell them exactly what it is we want from them. They will want to know about:

- the finance needed
- the repayment schedule
- the security available.

The finance needed

First, we must say what it is we want – a loan from the bank or investment from a would-be partner, as examples. We also need to state the exact amount. It is a good idea to ask for a little more than we might need rather than a little less. We should allow for an extra 10 per cent or so to allow for a margin of error in our calculations. A lender will not be impressed if we have to go back and ask for more in a month or two's time.

We should also state what we intend to use the money for (even if we think it might be obvious from what we have said before). We might need it to build an extra showroom alongside our existing premises, for example. We must remember to say when we need it. This might be before the business starts, for example.

A lender will also want to know how much we are putting in ourselves. Most lenders want to see some financial input from a prospective borrower as it shows their commitment to the business. If we are not committed to our business idea, we cannot really expect anyone else to be! As a rule, most lenders would expect an entrepreneur to put in the same amount of money as they are asking to borrow.

The repayment schedule

We should state when we are planning to repay our borrowings. This might be over 12 months or could be as long as 60 months for many borrowings. It is sensible to err on the side of caution. Too many entrepreneurs try to impress by promising repayments within 12 months. This puts unnecessary pressure on them and can damage relations with the lender if they cannot meet such a tight schedule.

We should also show the lender how we are going to make repayments. Our promises are meaningless without those hard facts and figures. We need to refer here to our profit budget, our cash-flow forecast and our projected annual accounts. We should have a margin of error built in so that we can still make repayments even if someone is late in paying us.

The security available

We will almost certainly want to make repayments from our business profits. But we need to address the worst-case scenario. How will we make repayments if everything goes wrong? This is the question that every reputable lender will ask. We need to be able to answer it convincingly. For example, we need to look to make repayments from selling assets or even remortgaging our home. As always, we need to back up what we are saying. If we have equity in our house, we need to get a valuation from estate agents and show our most recent mortgage statement.

Summary

We have spent Wednesday putting together the financial section of our business plan. Our reader will, in particular, want to see a profit budget outlining sales, direct costs, overheads and profits, along with explanatory notes and supporting documents. They will also want to see a cash-flow forecast detailing receipts, payments and balances, plus supporting notes and backup materials.

Whatever the main purpose of writing our business plan, we will also want to use these documents for ourselves. Is our business running at a profit, now and in the future? We may perhaps have a 'cash-rich' business that feels profitable but is making less profit than we thought when we crunch the numbers. Alternatively, we may, on paper, have a very profitable business but we can now see that, if we don't get some of the overdue cash in soon, we might struggle to pay the next quarter's rent!

Often, the annual accounts, in the form of a profit and loss account and a balance sheet, will reveal many 'home truths'. We may, in the light of these, want to think again about our financial requirements in terms of the finance needed and the proposed repayment schedule. Some entrepreneurs try to pay back too much too soon. See what the numbers tell you.

SUNDAY

MONDAY

TUESDAY

WEDNESDAY

THURSDAY

FRIDAY

SATURDAY

Fact-check [answers at the back]

We can check our knowledge of what we've worked through today by answering these multiple-choice questions and then comparing what we put with the answers at the end of the book.

1. What should a profit budget reveal about a firm's finances?
   a) Whether it is trading profitably ☐
   b) When it is short of cash ☐
   c) Whether it has plenty of cash ☐
   d) Whether it is trading at a loss ☐

2. Which figure tells us if our firm is truly profitable?
   a) The bank account balance ☐
   b) The gross profit figure ☐
   c) The trading profit figure ☐
   d) The gross profit margin ☐

3. What should a cash-flow forecast reveal about a firm's finances?
   a) The firm's cash position at any given time ☐
   b) When it has plenty of cash ☐
   c) When it is short of cash ☐
   d) The firm's profit or loss position at any given time ☐

4. What might we find in the cash-flow forecast's backup materials?
   a) Loan agreement forms ☐
   b) Suppliers' terms of sale ☐
   c) Our own comments and statements ☐
   d) Comments and statements from independent sources ☐

5. What period of time would a profit and loss account normally cover?
   a) One month ☐
   b) One quarter ☐
   c) Six months ☐
   d) One year ☐

6. What should the contents of a profit and loss account be based upon?
   a) Invoiced income and expenditure ☐
   b) Estimated cash incomings and outgoings ☐
   c) Actual cash incomings and outgoings ☐
   d) Opening and closing bank balances ☐

7. What does the balance sheet show?
   a) Opening and closing bank balances ☐
   b) Assets and liabilities ☐
   c) Profits and losses ☐
   d) Opening and closing cash positions ☐

8. What should we include when writing about the finance needed?
   a) How much we want to borrow ☐
   b) What we intend to use it for ☐
   c) How much we are putting in ourselves ☐
   d) When we expect to come back to ask for more ☐

9. As a rule of thumb, how much would a lender expect us to invest in relation to the proposed borrowings?

a) Twice as much ☐
b) About the same ☐
c) Half as much ☐
d) Nothing at all ☐

10. What do we need to refer to when setting out the proposed repayment schedule?

a) Our profit budget ☐
b) Our cash-flow forecast ☐
c) Our profit and loss account ☐
d) Our bank account statements ☐

SUNDAY

MONDAY

TUESDAY

WEDNESDAY

THURSDAY

FRIDAY

SATURDAY

THURSDAY

Adding the appendices

Today we are going to sort out the appendices. This is a relatively easy task. On one side, we have our commercial and financial sections. On the other, we have a big pile of materials and documents that are going to back up all of the key facts and figures given in the commercial and financial sections.

What we have to do is to go back through the commercial section and, as and when we come across something that needs to be backed up by an independent source, we then go through the mass of backup materials to find something to support it. We can then repeat the process with the financial section. We will probably want to tweak and tidy these sections as we go along.

Once we have our appendices in some sort of order, we will probably want to tidy them up further so that these are, like the commercial and financial sections, presented in a clear, professional manner. None of this is difficult. It just takes time. There's lots to do today...

- selecting the documents
- preparing the documents
- completing the appendices.

Selecting the documents

When we wrote our commercial and financial sections, we considered those documents which supported our various comments and details. We now need to read back over what we stated so that we can pick the right documents for inclusion in our appendices. Let's consider again:

- our business
- our products and services
- our team
- our market
- our finances.

Our business

Here, we might want to have copies of annual accounts, the business transfer agent's particulars, an accountant's assessment and any positive newspaper and magazine cuttings about our firm. A map might also be put in to indicate the firm's location and surroundings. With regard to the premises, equipment, machinery and vehicles, we might enclose photographs or scale drawings (or both), the estate agent's details, copies of the freehold deeds or leasehold agreement, the solicitor's comments, a surveyor's report, and copies of planning-permission documents, sales documents and hire-purchase agreements, as relevant. Copies of our website pages may be useful additions, too.

Our products and services

To substantiate and enhance the data given about our goods and services, we could incorporate samples or photographs as appropriate, production schedules, suppliers' price lists, independent test results plus our own price guides, sales literature, and advertising and other promotional materials. We might then put in the same (or abbreviated) information about our rivals' products and services.

Our team

The information that we gave about our team – us, our colleagues and our employees – can be backed up by including curricula vitae, copies of certificates and diplomas, newspaper, magazine or online features, and copies of either the partnership-agreement or company-formation documents, as relevant. It is important to support any legal papers with a solicitor's letter explaining these. Estimates of professional fees to be incurred for work done externally rather than in-house would be useful additions, too.

Our market

To back up the details provided about our customers, competitors and the marketplace, we should think about putting in a map highlighting their respective locations, along with customer sales records, orders and any research findings we have obtained about our customers. For our competitors, we could include materials similar to those used to substantiate facts and figures about our business – press cuttings, photographs and whatever else is available and relevant. Trade association reports about the marketplace may be helpful additions as well.

Our finances

Here, it would be a good idea to include proof of any capital available, quotes and estimates of costs and overheads, letters or other documentation from creditors and debtors confirming payment dates, and proof of security that can be put forward as and when loan facilities are provided. Not surprisingly, much of the supporting evidence we might put here will already have been included elsewhere – in customers' sales orders, for example.

We have talked a lot about what we should place in our appendices – and rightly so, because they are of crucial importance. It may be beneficial at this point to look at the following checklist, ticking off those items we intend to incorporate, and perhaps adding others, as relevant to us:

- annual accounts
- business transfer/estate agent's particulars
- accountant's comments
- newspaper/magazine cuttings and/or online features about the business, products, team, etc.
- photographs/drawings of premises, equipment, machinery, products, etc.
- copies of freehold deeds/leasehold agreement, plus solicitor's comments
- surveyor's report
- copies of planning permission
- sales documents/hire-purchase agreements
- website pages
- product samples
- production schedules
- suppliers' price lists
- independent test results
- our price guides, sales, advertising and promotional literature
- data on rival goods and services
- curricula vitae
- copies of partnership-agreement/company-formation documents, with solicitor's comments

- customer-sales records and orders
- customer-research findings
- data about competitors
- trade-association reports
- proof of capital
- quotes/estimates of costs and overheads
- creditors'/debtors' letters
- proof of security
- anything else you can think of that's relevant to you.

Preparing the documents

Some of our documents may be complex and lengthy in nature, and the reader will need help to find the key information in them. To assist the reader here, let's take a look at what we can do to improve our:

- external documents
- internal documents.

External documents

The external documents that we are going to put in our appendices might come from a wide variety of different sources, such as these:

accountants	European government
business transfer agents	media
estate agents	solicitors
chambers of commerce	suppliers
colleges and universities	surveyors
customers	trade bodies
local government	the Internet
national government	

Wherever possible, we should try to include the original documents, unless they are especially valuable or difficult to replace. The originals are always more believable than photocopies, which have sometimes been used to disguise altered documentation. Copies of the originals should be retained for our own records, though.

It is sensible to study each externally supplied item in turn – sales literature, accounts, press clippings or whatever – to decide which parts are most relevant to our text and of interest to the reader. Highlight these areas with a marker pen to focus the reader's attention on them and away from other, less relevant information.

Where necessary, be prepared to add an explanatory comment at the side or bottom of a page – a definition of a trade expression, an interpretation of a set of figures, or the date of an unmarked magazine article. We must always bear in mind who is reading our business plan and amend our text to suit them – after all, they may not know as much as we do, or indeed anything about our activities at all.

With lengthier items such as a lease or trading accounts for several years, it can be useful to attach a summary of the key facts, for easy reference. This should be set out on a point-by-point basis, and be as brief and concise as possible. Hard facts, rather than opinions, should be put across: the reader can reach an opinion of their own.

Internal documents

Some of the documents that are going into the appendices will come from in-house sources or will be put together by outsiders acting upon our instructions. We might obtain such assorted documents from:

- our own books and records
- our website
- the finance department
- the purchasing department
- the personnel department
- the production department
- the marketing department
- the administration department
- printers
- photographers
- illustrators.

Existing documents

It is advisable again to put in the originals, even if they are scruffy and perhaps completed in an idiosyncratic manner. Obviously, a messy set of sales records is not ideal, but at least they are real and believable, and far better than those which look false and artificial because they have been rewritten in a new book. And again, we need to highlight key areas, and add explanatory notes and a summary of important facts, if necessary, to make the reading that much easier for our recipient.

New documents

There will be materials which we can personally compose for this business plan – most notably, curricula vitae, scale drawings of our premises and a summary of customer research findings. Perhaps we surveyed our customers to discover their purchasing habits and opinions. It is sensible to make sure that these documents match the overall, professional image of the rest of the plan, being attractive, easy to understand, realistic and so on. The dos and don'ts of writing a commercial and a financial section apply just as much to the appendices, whenever possible.

Remaining items that may be prepared for us upon our suggestions might include photographs or illustrations (or both) of business premises and goods, sales, advertising and promotional material, and legal documents such as partnership agreements. Evidently, we need to make it absolutely clear what we want and why, but after that we should allow ourselves to be guided by the photographer, illustrator or whoever. After all, we will be paying for their expertise, so we should certainly make the most of it.

Completing the appendices

Now that we have selected and prepared our documents, we must complete the appendices by deciding upon their:

- individual order
- overall position
- general accessibility.

Individual order

It is advisable to put the documents in the same order that they were referred to in the commercial and financial sections. Thus, the reader can simply look at each in sequence, referring back to an earlier item as and when required. Avoid the temptation to bring neater and more attractive items to the front and hide other, messy documents at the back, since this will only bewilder and confuse the reader.

Overall position

If we have relatively few documents to include, our appendices can be placed after the commercial and financial sections, all together in the same file. On the other hand, should there be many lengthy or bulky items, it is better to put them in a separate file or folder. Ideally, this should be marked 'Appendices', and will match the main file in order to uphold that essential, professional image.

General accessibility

We must provide a list of our appendices somewhere to help the reader who wants to dip in and out as appropriate. If our appendices have been slotted in at the back of the main file, we can detail numbers, titles and pages for the various documents at the bottom of our contents page.

If, however, we have placed our appendices in a second file or folder, we could add something along the lines of 'Our appendices are in the accompanying file' to the contents page and then affix a list of numbers, titles and pages to the front of this backup folder. It all makes it that much easier for the reader to find their way around!

Just to add that final touch, we can attach white page-number stickers to the top right corner of each page of the appendices – 'Appendix 6: Estate Agent's Letter: Page 17', 'Appendix 6: Continued: Page 18' and so forth. This enables the reader to find the exact page they want, almost instantly.

Summary

We're now at the stage of the week where our business plan is falling nicely into place. We have been through our commercial and financial sections again and decided what we need to put into the appendices to back up our stated facts and figures. (We've probably also seen one or two parts of the text where we can trim and tidy things up a little.)

What we focused on doing today was to select the right documents to support our comments about our business, products and services, team, market and finances. Hopefully, these are from independent sources, where possible – the more independent, the better.

To create a professional image, we have also prepared our external and internal documents so that they may be found and read easily. This plan is being written for our reader so we want them to be able to check forwards and backwards, cross-referencing everything quickly. We have completed the appendices by sorting out their individual order, overall position and general accessibility for the reader.

SUNDAY

MONDAY

TUESDAY

WEDNESDAY

THURSDAY

FRIDAY

SATURDAY

Fact-check [answers at the back]

Let's double-check what we've done today by working through these multiple-choice questions. When we have answered them, we can check the correct answers at the end of the book.

1. What might we include to back up what we've written in the 'Our business' section?
a) A map of the location and surroundings ❏
b) A scale drawing of the premises ❏
c) Curricula vitae for ourselves and employees ❏
d) Samples of rivals' products ❏

2. What might be seen in the 'Our team' section of the appendices?
a) Company-formation documents ❏
b) A partnership agreement ❏
c) Curricula vitae ❏
d) Birth certificates ❏

3. What might we include to support what we've put in the 'Our market' section?
a) Suppliers' price lists ❏
b) A leasehold agreement ❏
c) Customers' sales records ❏
d) Customers' sales orders ❏

4. When it comes to externally produced documents, what should we include in the appendices?
a) Originals, where possible ❏
b) Only photocopies ❏
c) Only summaries of key facts ❏
d) Our opinions of them, whenever possible ❏

5. What sort of information might we write into the sidebars of a detailed document?
a) A definition of a trade expression ❏
b) Our phone number ❏
c) An artistic doodle to catch the eye ❏
d) The date of an unmarked magazine article ❏

6. What can we do to improve messy and unclear, internally produced documents for the appendices?
a) Highlight key points with a marker pen ❏
b) Add explanatory comments, where relevant ❏
c) Attach a summary of key facts ❏
d) Nothing – leave them messy and unclear ❏

7. What documents might we create personally and specifically for this business plan's appendices?
a) Photographs of our goods ❏
b) Business cards ❏
c) Customer research findings ❏
d) Scale drawings of our premises ❏

8. In what order should we put our appendices?
a) Alphabetical order ❏
b) As referred to in the commercial and financial sections ❏
c) Neatest at the front, messiest at the back ❏
d) No particular order at all ❏

9. Where should lengthy and bulky appendices be placed?
a) All together after the commercial section ❏
b) All together after the commercial and financial sections ❏
c) Individually, as they are referred to in the commercial and financial sections ❏
d) In a separate file or folder, marked accordingly ❏

10. What can we do to make our appendices more readily accessible to the reader?
a) Provide a contents list upfront ❏
b) Number and title each appendix, as relevant ❏
c) Attach numbered and titled white stickers to each appendix ❏
d) Exclude the lengthiest and bulkiest ones ❏

SUNDAY

MONDAY

TUESDAY

WEDNESDAY

THURSDAY

FRIDAY

SATURDAY

FRIDAY

Submitting a business plan

Today we want to approach the reader, whether that's a bank or a would-be investor, about our business plan. If the plan is all ready to go, we may want to submit it straightaway and arrange a meeting in a week or so to discuss it. If we think it could still do with a tweak or two, we may want to get in touch with the reader to say it's on its way soon.

Nowadays almost everyone has a computer and we will almost certainly – except where a bank has asked us to fill in one of their ready-made forms – have prepared everything on screen, usually in word.doc format. Many entrepreneurs assume they will simply submit everything as an email attachment. That's not always ideal – we cannot, as an example, always include samples of our goods easily online! And copying and attaching lots of material for our appendices is not an easy task.

As we will have done with all parts of the plan, we should ask ourselves what the reader wants. The chances are that, even if we submit online, they will want a hard copy so that they can sit and read through it, and make notes in the margins etc. Rather than expect them to print everything off, it's better if we do it for them. So, today, we are going to work through...

- writing an introductory letter
- delivering the plan
- preparing for a meeting.

Writing an introductory letter

It is courteous to send an introductory letter, either by post or by email, ahead of, or with, a business plan which is going to be studied by someone from outside our organization, such as a bank or would-be investor. As a first point of contact, this letter should convey an impression of smooth professionalism. If we can achieve this, the recipient may be more inclined, or even keen, to read our entire plan. Thus, we need to think carefully about the letter's:

- appearance
- contents
- style.

Appearance

If the letter is posted separately in advance of a plan being delivered in person, then we need to begin by considering the **envelope**. A scruffy, dog-eared one with a misspelled name or address is not going to put the reader in a favourable mood towards us. We need to choose a top-quality envelope which matches the enclosed paper, rather than a nondescript buff one. The recipient's *correct* name, job title, address and postcode should be printed carefully in the centre of the front of the envelope. A rubber stamp of our firm's name or logo, imprinted at the top left opposite the first-class stamp, adds a classy touch.

Letterheaded and watermarked A4 **paper** is a must if we want to be taken seriously. Similarly, a typed letter is more formal and professional in appearance than a handwritten one; the text itself has to look neat and easy to read. Generous margins to the top, sides and bottom of the page are helpful, as are short paragraphs of equal length. Tidy and error-free **text** is just as important: incorrectly spelled or missed-out words make us look careless and amateurish – we should always *rewrite* a letter rather than post it off with any flaws.

Contents

At the top of the page, we should have our **letterhead**, incorporating the firm's name, address, telephone number, fax number, email address and/or website and logo, as relevant. Next, we should type in the **date** of our letter, putting '17 May 2012' rather than '17th May 2012' or an abbreviation such as '17-5-12' or '17/5/12' which looks sloppy. Under this, we need to detail the **reader's name, job title and address**. If in *any* doubt, we should check these out – especially their sex, their initials and the precise spelling of their surname. Making a mistake here could irritate or cause offence.

Following on, we must **greet the reader by name**, rather than by 'Dear Sir' or 'Dear Madam', which conveys the unfortunate impression that this is no more than a circular being sent out to anybody and everyone! Below our greeting of 'Dear Mr di Carlo', 'Dear Ms Thomson' or whatever, we can indicate the **subject matter** of the letter by putting 'Re:' and a heading which sums up what we are writing about. We could underline this for emphasis if we wish.

Then we come to the **main part** of our letter. Typically, we might say who we are and what our business is, if the recipient is likely to be unaware of these points. Moving on, we can then explain the plan itself and say why we have drawn it up and sent it (or why we are *going* to send it) to them. It can be helpful to outline what will happen next – the plan will arrive tomorrow, we will make an appointment to see them in a week's time, or whatever. We need to keep this brief and to the point. It is an introductory letter, and no more. All of the key information is in the business plan, so we do not have to repeat anything here.

After this, we should **end our letter** with 'Yours sincerely' or the less formal 'Kind regards' or 'Best regards', as preferred. It is sensible to provide a clear, readable signature rather than one adorned with swirls and embellishments or a rushed and careless squiggle – neither type will impress. Finally, we should add our name and job title, if relevant. 'Enc.' or 'Enclosure' can also be put on a letter if it is being submitted with the business plan itself.

Style

As with the commercial and financial sections of our plan, the letter has to be clear and easy to understand. We must use language to suit the recipient – perhaps technical for a fellow expert, and simplified for a non-specialist. Short words, phrases and sentences tend to be unambiguous and are less likely to be misinterpreted. In-house slang, local expressions and personal quirks all increase the possibility of misunderstandings.

It is worth stressing here that the letter must be concise. We are simply introducing ourselves and our business plan – not trying to give our life history or details of all the ins and outs of the plan. We should therefore check over what we have written, asking ourselves whether the points we have made are relevant to the recipient. If they are not, we must eliminate them. Then, we need to consider whether we have set out those key points as briefly as we can, watching out for waffle or repetition.

Here is a checklist we can use when writing our letter:

- a top-quality envelope, matching the paper
- the correct name, job title, address and postcode of the recipient on the envelope
- a rubber stamp of our firm's name or logo
- a first-class stamp; it's a first-class proposal!
- Letterheaded and watermarked A4 paper
- typed, not handwritten; we're professionals!
- neat and easy-to-read text, using suitable language
- tidy, error-free text, concise and to the point
- the date
- the reader's name, job title and address – correct again!
- a personal greeting – not 'Dear Sir' or 'Dear Madam'
- the subject matter, 'Re:'
- the main text – who we are, what our business is, etc.
- 'Yours sincerely' or similar
- a clear, readable signature
- our name and job title
- 'Enclosure', if appropriate.

It may be useful to look at a simple example of a good introductory letter:

Gayther Plumbing and Heating Services
76 The Road, Padbury, Sussex ME12 3BB
Tel/Fax: 01724 994312
Email: gayther@nvc.com

14 July 2012

Mr B. Stone
The Manager
Padbury Bank plc
72 High Street
Padbury
Sussex
ME11 6BT

Dear Mr Stone

Re: Brightwell's

I am a self-employed plumber who wishes to buy the Brightwell's shop at 64 High Street, Padbury.

As I require some financial assistance to purchase and develop this going concern, I am writing to ask if Padbury Bank would consider helping me. A business plan detailing all relevant information is enclosed for your attention.

I have booked an appointment for 11 o'clock on 22 July so that we can discuss this matter in more detail.

I look forward to meeting you.

Yours sincerely,

John Gayther

John Gayther

Enclosure

Delivering the plan

Many people spend ages putting together a first-rate business plan but then fail to deliver it properly. It needs to reach the recipient in an excellent condition in order to create that professional image we are seeking to convey. Just as important, it must arrive *on time*, especially if we are going to the bank in a week or so: they have to be given sufficient time to study the material in depth, think of questions and draw conclusions before our meeting. There are various ways of delivering our plan:

- by post
- in person
- via an intermediary
- via email.

By post

Posting the business plan may be a necessity – perhaps we are trying to raise finance to start a business some distance from where we live, and are approaching an investor in that area. If so, we need to make sure that it is wrapped securely – an apparently obvious point but it is not unknown for plans with bulky appendices to burst apart during transit. Not only does this put across a rather shabby image, but it could also damage the business plan itself, making it difficult to read. It is also sensible to send it by registered post so that delivery is guaranteed on a particular day. A registered delivery has an aura of importance about it, too – just what we want!

Submitting our business plan by post is probably not the ideal method of delivery, though – after all, once it is out of our hands, we have lost control and something could go wrong. Even if nothing goes wrong, we will still be worrying about it for a day or so and making unnecessary (and potentially irritating) phone calls to check its safe arrival.

In person

Clearly, the safest way of getting our plan to the person in an excellent condition and on time is to give it to them personally. If we speak to their secretary or whoever in advance, our neat and tidy file or folders can be taken in when we know that they are free and perhaps have an hour or so available to look through our material.

Making sure that we ourselves appear equally neat and presentable, we should do no more at this point than introduce ourselves, explain why we are here and hand across the plan. We should end by saying that we look forward to hearing from them shortly or that we will make (or have made) an appointment to see them in a week's time. This may be wiser, especially if we want a reasonably prompt decision.

Of course, it is not always easy to simply say 'hello', hand over the business plan and then withdraw as we ought to do at this stage. We may be drawn into a conversation we are ill prepared for, or could be asked questions that we have not yet thought of or thought through. We might not put across the right image, and could even make fools of ourselves if we are nervous and tense.

Via an intermediary

Perhaps it is most sensible to leave our file or folders with an intermediary such as a receptionist, the recipient's secretary or personal assistant, or another responsible member of their staff. This way, we can present it in a professional manner, and know it has arrived and *when* it is likely to be seen by that recipient. Thus, we avoid the problems of packaging, postal damage or loss, and any potential embarrassment from a face-to-face encounter we have not prepared for fully.

Via email

These days many entrepreneurs will be looking to submit their business plan by email and, if this is how the reader wants to receive it, you can send in your plan as, typically, a word.doc attachment with, as relevant, a separate file for the appendices. However, it is important to double-check what the reader wants. Some banks, for example, still want you to fill in a form they provide and then hand that in. There are other issues with submitting a business plan by email – some entrepreneurs produce lavish plans in various formats which are not always easy to download on older systems. Also, appendices rarely comprise neat, A4 typed sheets that can be copied and attached easily. Sometimes, the 'old-fashioned' ways – a neat and tidy, hard-copy plan with appendices in a separate, bulkier file – can be the best.

Preparing for a meeting

Ideally, our business plan stands alone, containing all of the commercial and financial information and supporting materials necessary for the recipient to reach a decision – hopefully in our favour! Nevertheless, in most cases we will be expected to attend a meeting to discuss the plan and answer any questions relating to it. By arranging this meeting for a week or so after the plan has been delivered, we give the recipient a chance to read it, and ourselves sufficient time to prepare for this meeting.

When preparing, we should consider three areas in particular:

- our approach
- their questions
- our answers.

Our approach

We must make certain that our appearance is appropriate for the meeting. Smart dress is generally a sensible choice because it acknowledges the importance of the occasion, and shows our respect for the recipient of the business plan. Obviously, it does also depend largely on individual circumstances, though. If we know and are on friendly terms with the person, then we can wear whatever would be considered acceptable by them – 'smart but casual', for example. At the same time, however, we need to feel comfortable. A thick jacket, itchy new top, tight trousers and pinched shoes will feel uncomfortable and may distract us from the conversation.

How we speak is often regarded as being as important as our appearance. We must ensure that we are heard clearly, achieving this by holding up our head, opening our mouth wide and speaking out in a firm, strong voice. We need to sound confident, sure of our facts and enthusiastic, too – if we are not, *they* won't be either. Speaking slowly to emphasize key points can be a good idea as well.

Some thought should be given to our manner during the meeting. We must avoid seeming brash and overconfident, or nervous and servile at the other extreme. Ideally, we should be friendly and sincere and ready to answer any questions in a polite and positive way. We can help to convey this impression by looking interested throughout, leaning forward and maintaining eye contact and remaining fairly still at all times.

Their questions

Not surprisingly, our main worry when we are preparing to meet whoever has received our business plan concerns the questions we are likely to be asked. Generally, these questions fall into two broad categories:

1 those arising from the contents of the plan, *and*
2 those relating to the recipient's knowledge of external factors, which we may not know about.

Any questions regarding what we put in the commercial and financial sections will probably be asked to check facts, clarify vague or confusing text, or deal with any omissions. For example, we may not have mentioned a competitor that the recipient is aware of and respects. A good way of anticipating these questions is to let a trusted colleague see the plan and prepare dummy questions for us to answer. It is also sensible to read fully through the business plan just before the meeting to remind ourselves of exactly what we stated and why.

Most of the questions raised will simply seek confirmation of or further information about what we have stated – Why did we put this or that? Is this realistic? What would happen if that payment was not received on time? – and so forth. We should be able to handle these comfortably if we know what we are doing, have anticipated the questions in advance and thought of our replies. Unfortunately, there may be one or two questions dealing with issues we do not know about, such as a new competitor who is to start trading soon. These are harder to predict and handle, and so we need to think about how we are going to answer any tricky questions *before* we go into that meeting.

Our answers

When we are asked a question during the meeting, our answer should be an honest one even if it reveals a problem or a lack of knowledge about something. The recipient will not expect this to be a perfect proposal – simply because such a proposal doesn't exist – and may be happy to help address a difficulty or add to our understanding. They will certainly be more impressed by our honesty than by a waffly response or an obvious lie which would damage our reputation.

If a problem becomes apparent, we should face it, outline our plans for tackling it (or at least coping with it) and then ask for the recipient's opinion. 'What do you think?' flatters the recipient, puts them in a positive mood towards us and may even produce a possible solution. Should we be unaware of the answer to a particular question, we should say something like, 'I'm sorry, I don't know, but I'll find out and let you know'. Alternatively, we could reply with 'I'm sorry, I don't know. What information do you have?' if it seems likely that the recipient understands the situation.

Generally, everything we say during this meeting must be brief and to the point – we should adopt the attitude that the recipient's time is valuable and that we do not want to waste any of it. Our comments and responses must be easy to understand, too – we should use simple words, sentences and phrases which are suited to the recipient's level of knowledge and understanding of the subject matter.

Naturally enough, what we have to say has to be realistic rather than hopeful – most banks and other would-be investors have heard it all before and will be distinctly unimpressed by pipe dreams. We should refer, when necessary, to backup materials in the appendices. Again, a bank wants hard facts, not ifs, buts and maybes.

Summary

We should be able to look back over what we've done today and say to ourselves that we have found out how the reader wanted to receive our business plan and that we have delivered it in that format; whether that is online or offline. The reader may, for example, have wanted the basic plan sent by email with appendices being brought in later to a meeting. If so, that is how we should have done it.

Generally, we have, today, written an introductory letter with appropriate appearance, contents and style. We have then delivered the plan by post, in person, via an intermediary or online. Job done? Nearly, but not quite!

We will usually have to attend a meeting to discuss the business plan and answer any questions that the reader may have. As such, we have prepared for a meeting by contemplating our approach and anticipating the recipient's questions and our answers. It is a good idea to show our business plan to someone we know and trust and who can act as if they are the reader. They will produce some questions and we need to be sure we can answer these effectively.

SUNDAY

MONDAY

TUESDAY

WEDNESDAY

THURSDAY

FRIDAY

SATURDAY

Fact-check [answers at the back]

We can check Friday's work by answering these multiple-choice questions. We can then compare what we've put with the correct answers that are given at the end of the book.

1. When writing an introductory letter, what can we include so that it stands out from the crowd?
   a) A top-quality envelope ❏
   b) A rubber-stamped business logo ❏
   c) Headed and watermarked A4 paper ❏
   d) Neatly handwritten text, carefully corrected where relevant ❏

2. When writing our greeting, what should we use? ❏
   a) 'Dear Sir', if a man ❏
   b) 'Dear Madam', if a woman ❏
   c) 'Dear Sir or Madam', if we are not quite sure ❏
   d) Their correct title and name ❏

3. Style-wise, what does our introductory letter need to be?
   a) Warmly humorous, but not too amusing ❏
   b) Clear and easy to understand ❏
   c) Concise, with key points only ❏
   d) Full of impressive technical details ❏

4. How should a business plan be posted?
   a) By first class post ❏
   b) Well wrapped ❏
   c) Not too bulky ❏
   d) By registered post ❏

5. What is the main aim of delivering a plan by hand?
   a) To hand over a plan in excellent condition ❏
   b) To tell whoever we meet as much about the plan as possible ❏
   c) To impress whoever we meet with our know-how and expertise ❏
   d) To ask for money while we've got the chance ❏

6. When it comes to delivering our plan by email, what should be our main concern?
   a) That we deliver it in an impressive format, such as pdf ❏
   b) That the reader thinks we are computer literate ❏
   c) That we showcase the best bits of our business ❏
   d) That we deliver the business plan in the way the reader most wants to receive it ❏

7. What should our approach to a meeting to discuss the business plan include?
   a) Dressing smartly to suit the occasion ❏
   b) Speaking slowly and in a clear voice ❏
   c) Providing technical information to impress ❏
   d) Being friendly and sincere ❏

8. What are the best ways to prepare to answer questions about the plan?
a) Read through the plan ourselves to identify possible questions ❏
b) Ask a trusted colleague to read the plan and ask us questions ❏
c) Wait for the reader to ask questions and have a go at them on the spot ❏
d) Wait for the reader to ask questions and ask that we can respond to them later in writing ❏

9. How should we respond to a question we can't immediately answer?
a) Make something up and sound as convincing as possible ❏
b) Waffle vaguely to distract them ❏
c) Say we don't know but will find out ❏
d) Say we don't know and ask for their thoughts ❏

10. What does the person we're meeting expect us to be like?
a) Forceful and ready to argue our case to get the money ❏
b) Brief and to the point ❏
c) Full of trade jargon to show we know what's what ❏
d) Realistic ❏

SUNDAY

MONDAY

TUESDAY

WEDNESDAY

THURSDAY

FRIDAY

SATURDAY

SATURDAY

Presenting a business plan

We come to the last day of the week: our plan has been submitted to the reader, in the way they want it, and we can sit back and wait for the thumbs-up. Yes? Maybe, but not necessarily!

It may be that a decision – hopefully a positive one – will be made purely on the basis of what we have sent in. But, especially if we are not known to the reader or there are various questions that need to be answered, we may well have to attend a meeting to discuss what's in the plan.

Having submitted our business plan to the bank or whoever, we need to be ready to present it to them at a meeting where they will ask questions and we will have to answer. Make or break? Possibly – but if we are well prepared, we should be well placed to get whatever it is we want. Remember, if the meeting is taking place, the reader should be close to acceptance, subject to one or two questions. They would not waste their time on a meeting if they were planning to say no. Even so, we still have some work to do...

- attending a meeting
- receiving a response
- reviewing our activities.

Attending a meeting

If the meeting that we arranged a week or so ago is going ahead, this is a very good sign: it indicates that the recipient has studied the plan and is in favour of it, or is at least open to persuasion. If they were unimpressed, we would almost certainly have heard from them by now with a rejection letter, email or phone call.

We can view the meeting as involving three distinct stages:

- the beginning
- the middle
- the end.

The beginning

Perhaps the most important piece of advice to be given here – and it is not always followed – is simply to *turn up on time*. There is nothing more likely to annoy the recipient than being kept waiting. If they are, they may be in a rotten mood and we will have less time to discuss our plan. Some entrepreneurs go so far as to make the journey the day before to see how long it takes to get there!

Even if we do not feel it, we should try to appear calm and confident when we walk in, introducing ourselves to the receptionist or whoever is going to announce our arrival to the recipient. We must be prepared to smile, make eye contact and shake hands with the recipient when we come face to face with them. Small talk about the weather and our journey may have to be made as well.

When entering the room, we should wait to be shown to our seat rather than sitting down straight away: we may choose the wrong seat, which would be embarrassing for us. We should also decline politely any offer of a drink or biscuit. These are all potential dangers to us: we could splutter, choke or cough over them, which is distracting and even at times humiliating. It is best to sit there smiling, waiting for them to start talking.

The middle

However long the meeting lasts – perhaps 15 to 30 minutes – most of the time will be taken up by the recipient working through the business plan and asking questions about the commercial section, financial section and so on. Hopefully, we will have anticipated all of the questions and can answer them succinctly, either providing an explanation, promising to find out about something, or asking the recipient what they know about a particular subject.

It is often a sensible idea to take a notebook and pen or a laptop into the meeting with us. Not only does this give us something to do with our hands which we might otherwise wave about nervously, but it also makes us look professional. We can jot down useful points made by the recipient, add notes about any other work we have to do, and so forth.

Perhaps surprisingly, we should have a hard copy of the business plan with us, too. It is not unknown for a would-be investor to pull apart a plan and circulate extracts of it to colleagues for their opinions. Sometimes, these are not returned in time for our meeting. If we have full and complete information to hand, then it all helps to make us seem very professional and in control.

The end

Hopefully, a decision will be made towards the end of the meeting, or an indication of the likely decision will at least be given, subject to confirmation by the recipient's superiors in some cases. If, however, it is not forthcoming, we should not press for it as this can cause embarrassment or even offence. We should simply allow the recipient to draw the meeting to a conclusion, thank them for seeing us, smile and leave in a pleasant and friendly manner.

After the meeting, we could send a polite letter to the recipient thanking them again for meeting us and stating that we look forward to hearing from them within a certain length of time, typically one to two weeks at most. This is courteous and it puts a time limit on their decision. After all, if they are going to reject it, we want to take the plan elsewhere, and soon!

Receiving a response

If a decision has not been announced by the close of our meeting – perhaps because the business plan has to be forwarded to someone else for approval – we would expect to receive either a formal, written response or a more informal phone call from the recipient within the following week or so. We then need to deal with the consequences of one of the following:

- rejection
- acceptance.

Rejection

A plan which is turned down and returned to us by a potential source of finance, investment or assistance should not just be delivered automatically to the next name and address on our list of prospective lenders or whoever. There may be room for improvement. We should try to discover *why* it was rejected by studying the letter of rejection. Or we can phone or email the recipient for an explanation, if that would be considered acceptable – in some instances, it will be: after all, we should be entitled to a short explanation after all the time and effort we have put into our plan. However, to obtain a full and honest explanation, we must maintain our professionalism and not attempt to persuade them to change their mind. Their decision has been made, and that's that.

It may be that they think the proposition is not a viable one or at least is not for them. In either case, we should take note of their comments, sit down and review carefully our whole plan and its future prospects. At best, we will probably need to make some changes and improvements to it. At worst, it may be best not to proceed at all. Only we can decide what to do.

Hopefully, we will decide to continue and send the revised business plan elsewhere – to a lender who has a better knowledge of our market, or an investor who is also prepared to become involved in the day-to-day running of the firm, or whoever. Prior to resubmitting it, however, we should replace any pages which have become torn or grubby, remove references included for the last recipient's benefit, and amend outdated text, facts and figures. We need to convince the new recipient that the plan has been written especially for them, and that they are the first person to receive it,

Acceptance

At some stage, and perhaps even the first time around, our proposal will be accepted and we will be offered a loan from a bank, capital from a partner or a leasehold agreement from a landlord, or whatever it is we wanted. We can now celebrate, albeit briefly, before getting down to business again to expand, diversify or whatever, and go on to greater success in the future. But note: this does not mean we put away our business plan and forget all about it – in fact, quite the opposite.

Reviewing our activities

We are now going to look back over the week and review our activities day by day. Let's just remind ourselves what we studied each day:

Sunday	Understanding business plans
Monday	Making preparatory notes
Tuesday	Composing the commercial section
Wednesday	Compiling the financial section
Thursday	Adding the appendices
Friday	Submitting a business plan
Saturday	Presenting a business plan

Sunday

On Sunday, we found out all we needed to know about business plans:

● They usually contain commercial and financial sections, and are supported by appendices which verify and enhance these.
● They can be used to raise finance, attract investment, encourage assistance and improve performance.
● A successful business plan is well researched, adapted, attractive, understandable, realistic and backed up by independent evidence.

Monday

During Monday, we made some preparatory notes by conducting internal research, using external sources and accumulating appropriate information. This meant:

- drawing on our own extensive knowledge
- talking to our colleagues in other departments
- referring to company books and records
- contacting outside individuals and organizations such as banks, accountants, solicitors and the media
- approaching other external bodies as diverse as architects, photographers and market research companies
- jotting down notes under the headings 'The business', 'Products and services', 'The team', 'The market', 'Objectives', 'Finance' and 'Appendices'.

Tuesday

This was the day that we composed the commercial section of the plan. We included various ingredients:

- the preliminaries – title page, contents page, introduction
- our business – background, location, premises
- our products and services – features, selling points
- our team – ourselves, colleagues, employees
- the market – customers, competitors
- our objectives – short, medium and long term.

Wednesday

On Wednesday, we compiled the financial section of our business plan. We incorporated:

- a profit budget outlining sales, direct costs, overheads and profits, with explanatory notes and supporting documents
- a cash-flow forecast detailing receipts, payments and balances, with supplementary notes and backup materials
- annual accounts in the form of a profit and loss account and a balance sheet
- our financial requirements, and in particular the finance needed, the repayment schedule and the security available.

Thursday

During Thursday, we added appendices to our commercial and financial sections. We selected and prepared documents before completing these appendices. This involved:

- picking the right documents to substantiate the information given about our business, products and services, team, market and finances
- tidying up external documents to make them easy to look at
- producing internal documents which were understandable and simple to study
- putting the documents in the right order and position, and making them accessible.

Friday

This was the day that we dealt with submitting a business plan to a recipient. We considered:

- writing an introductory letter, paying special attention to its appearance, contents and style
- delivering the plan, either by post, in person, via an intermediary or by email
- preparing for a meeting with the recipient, with particular emphasis on our approach, their questions and our answers.

Saturday

Today we have had our busiest day. We have looked at how to present a business plan to the recipient, and have contemplated:
- attending a meeting, viewing this in terms of its beginning, middle and end
- receiving a response, discussing how to respond to a rejection or acceptance of our proposal
- all our activities to date, reviewing these on a step-by-step basis.

Summary

Writing a business plan is a key skill and to acquire it in a week is a considerable achievement – even more so if we go on and put together a successful plan that raises the finance or whatever it is we need.

However, it is important that we do not, once we have got the money, put away the plan and forget all about it as so many entrepreneurs are inclined to do. The fact is that the plan's most important role is yet to come. We need to keep working on it, continually comparing our budgeted and actual performances, especially with regard to profits and cash flows.

We need to learn from our errors and build on our successes so that we can make constant, ongoing use of this essential business tool, amending and developing it as and when necessary. Our plan can help to keep us in business, to improve and grow, and to make more sales and profits – everything we need to do this is here in front of us in our business plan.

We have come to the end of the week but this should not be the end of our business plan. Instead, this should be the beginning of our use, week in and week out, of our business plan.

SUNDAY

MONDAY

TUESDAY

WEDNESDAY

THURSDAY

FRIDAY

SATURDAY

Fact-check [answers at the back]

Almost done! We just need to go over our final day's work by answering these multiple-choice questions. We can then, for the final time, compare our answers with those provided at the end of the book.

1. When we enter the room for a meeting about our business plan, what should we do?
   a) Wait to be shown to a seat ❑
   b) Sit in the seat nearest to us ❑
   c) Accept their offer of a sweet ❑
   d) Smile and wait for the conversation to begin ❑

2. What should we take into the meeting with us?
   a) A packet of cigarettes ❑
   b) A notebook and pen ❑
   c) A copy of the business plan ❑
   d) Previously unsubmitted parts of the plan ❑

3. What should we do at the end of the meeting?
   a) Ask them for a decision now ❑
   b) Request at least an assessment of the proposal ❑
   c) Tell them how long they've got to make up their mind ❑
   d) Thank them and leave ❑

4. What should we do if the plan is rejected?
   a) Tell them they've made a mistake and explain why ❑
   b) Ask them politely for the reasons why ❑
   c) Deliver the plan as soon as possible to the next name on your list ❑
   d) Review the plan and rewrite it accordingly ❑

5. Before resubmitting the plan elsewhere, what do we need to do?
   a) Make changes based on feedback from any earlier rejection ❑
   b) Amend outdated material ❑
   c) Keep all the previous references for the previous reader's benefit ❑
   d) Replace torn and grubby pages ❑

6. What do we do when our plan has been accepted?
   a) Celebrate, albeit briefly as we have work to do ❑
   b) Dispose of our business plan ❑
   c) Begin using our commercial section regularly ❑
   d) Start using our financial section regularly ❑

7. Now that the business plan has 'done its job', what is the most likely future use for it on an immediate and ongoing basis?
   a) No use at all ❑
   b) To raise further finance ❑
   c) To attract further investment ❑
   d) To improve business performance ❑

8. Which parts of the commercial section should we be reviewing regularly on, say, at least a quarterly basis?
a) Our profit budget ❏
b) Our market ❏
c) Our objectives ❏
d) Our cash-flow forecast ❏

9. Which parts of the financial section should we be reviewing most regularly on, say, a monthly basis?
a) Our annual accounts ❏
b) Our profit budget ❏
c) Our cash-flow forecast ❏
d) Our objectives ❏

10. When should we refer to the appendices to help improve business performance?
a) Not at all ❏
b) When we review and update the commercial section ❏
c) As we review and update the financial section ❏
d) When we want to produce another successful business plan ❏

Surviving in tough times

In tough economic times, it's hard to run a successful business, raise money and grow and expand your money-making activities. For example, in recent times many banks have tightened their lending criteria and it can be harder than ever to get that overdraft or start-up loan or funding to diversify into new products, services or markets. However, what you've read in this guide will help you to maximize your chances of success. Here are ten key tips that will help you succeed.

1 Create a business plan for yourself

When times are tough, you need to do all you can to keep your business going, on course and profitable, at all times. This is the first main role of your business plan – to clarify what you are doing, where you are going and how you are going to get there. You also need to know where you are at any given time. Forget the widespread perception that a business plan is only for raising finance – it's not. In the first instance, it's for you – and it's all about keeping you in business in tough times.

2 Do your budgets and forecasts regularly

How much profit have you made this quarter? What's your bank balance right now? These are questions that everyone in business needs to answer at any time, let alone during these hard economic days. What income is coming in this month? Is that a 'definite' or a 'maybe'? What do you have to pay out? Do you have the money in place to make those payments and still have some cash in hand? Do those profit budgets and cash-flow forecasts on an on-going basis – it's the only way to keep strict financial control.

3 Remember the 'What's in it for me?'

If you are writing a business plan for someone else, tell them what they want to know; and do it again and again. The bank that has tightened its lending criteria in the days following Northern Rock and, more recently, the EU crisis, is less interested in how much you want to borrow – it wants to know more about the security you can offer against any borrowings. Whatever you write, think about their point of view. These are difficult times – tell them what you're doing to stay in business and how you will repay their money on time.

4 Remember the importance of independent proof

Imagine someone came to you and invited you to invest in a scheme. They say they earn £100,000 a year and you could do the same if you invest in, let's say, their franchise. You'd probably have lots of questions. The first would be – or certainly should be – 'Can you show me proof of your earnings?' If they couldn't, you'd be much less likely to invest. (In fact, you'd be wise not to do so.) The principle is exactly the same when you go to a bank and say 'this, that and the other'. The bank's first thoughts? Where's the proof!

5 Always value a second, even a third, opinion

If you're an entrepreneur who does everything yourself, you probably aren't used to the idea of asking for opinions from others. It's a good idea at any time, and more so in tougher times. Getting a second opinion can range from talking to, say, the bank in advance to check on their current lending criteria, to taking advice from the local council on any new grants that may be available, through to getting someone to read your business plan before submitting it. Maybe it just reads as being too upbeat and optimistic right now!

6 Be realistic

Of course, you don't want to be too downbeat about what you're doing – but you do need to be very realistic these days. This needs to be shown in various ways – not being too optimistic with sales figures and not looking too far into their future with budgets, forecasts and objectives, as examples. Focus on the achievable.

7 Be open-minded

It's also a good idea to touch a little more on the 'ifs, buts and maybes' of what might happen (and how you will act) rather than setting out, as many do, one particular course and outcome that is going to happen come what may. Business rarely unfolds exactly as expected at any time so it's wise to show you are ready for all possibilities; not just to overcome them but to make money from them as well. Say a rival stops trading suddenly – how can you benefit from that?

8 Work through the worst-case scenarios

Relatively few businesses are immune to the downturn. All sorts of businesses have been closing down. Among those that are surviving – and even thriving – are ones that think ahead and plan ahead via a business plan. They know what might happen and how they will act – hopefully before rather than after – to profit from opportunities and avoid losses when things take a turn for the worse. So, what will you do if you lose customers, costs rise and so on? What's your worst-case scenario and how will you handle it? Your prospective partner wants to know. You do too!

9 Think differently

When times are tough, many entrepreneurs will say, 'Well, we're still in business so we must be doing something right.' Maybe, but you could possibly do it better by thinking, as some might say, 'outside the box'. This is a good time to review what you are doing and think of different ways to achieve what you want to do. Perhaps a bank won't lend money. Maybe it's time to look at alternative sources – a grant from the council, an investor recommended by an accountant, as examples.

10 Uncover the upside

The business world these days is very different from what it was even two or three years ago. Everyone will tell you it's tough and hard and difficult. All true enough. Even so, tough times should not be viewed solely in a negative way; indeed, they can, or should, force us to become even more professional and businesslike – to use a business plan more effectively, to work through our budgets and forecasts regularly, and to make our businesses leaner and streamlined and ready to look for new and different opportunities. This all stands us in good stead for the better times and bigger profits that lie ahead.

Answers

Sunday: 1a & d; 2a & d;
3b, c & d; 4b & c; 5d;
6c; 7a & c; 8a & c; 9c;
10b, c & d

Monday: 1a; 2a & c;
3b & d; 4a, b & c;
5b & c; 6a & c; 7a & b;
8a, b & c; 9b & d;
10a, b & c

Tuesday: 1a, c & d; 2c;
3a & d; 4a, b & d;
5a & d; 6a & d;
7a, b & c; 8a, b & c;
9c; 10a & d

Wednesday: 1a, b & d; 2c;
3a, b & c; 4a, b & d;
5d; 6a; 7b; 8a, b & c;
9b; 10a, b & c

Thursday: 1a & b;
2a, b & c; 3c & d;
4a; 5a & d; 6a, b & c;
7a, c & d; 8b;
9d; 10a, b & c

Friday: 1a, b & c; 2d;
3b & c; 4b, c & d; 5a;
6d; 7a, b & d; 8a & b;
9c & d; 10b & d

Saturday: 1a & d; 2b & c;
3d; 4b & d; 5a, b & d;
6a, c & d; 7d; 8b & c;
9b & c; 10b, c & d

Notes